SQUARE SUN SQUARE MOON

the world is round
the world is square
and you and I are
everywhere

reps

SQUARE
SUN
SQUARE
MOON

A Collection of Sweet Sour Essays

by PAUL REPS

CHARLES E. TUTTLE CO.: PUBLISHERS
Rutland, Vermont, U. S. A. & Tokyo, Japan

Representative

For Continental Europe:
BOXERBOOKS INC., *Zurich*

For the British Isles:
PRENTICE-HALL INTERNATIONAL INC., *London*

For Australasia:
PAUL FLESCH & CO., PTY. LTD., *Melbourne*

For Canada:
M. G. HURTIG LTD., *Edmonton*

Published by the Charles E. Tuttle Company, Inc.
of Rutland, Vermont & Tokyo, Japan
with editorial offices at Suido 1–chome, 2–6
Bunkyo–ku, Tokyo, Japan

Copyright in Japan, 1967 by Charles E. Tuttle Co., Inc.

Library of Congress Catalog Card No. 67–14277

Standard Book No. 8048 0544-x

First edition, 1967
Fourth printing, 1970

Book design by Keiko Chiba

Printed in Japan

PREFACE

Some of these writings have appeared in American Fabrics magazine, New York, USA and in Mainichi Daily News, Tokyo, Japan, to whom thanks, thanks.

All of them are about human experiences in China, Samoa, Tahiti, Fiji, Japan, Norway, Sweden and in the author.

Their viewpoint is personal, even intimate. So as far as I know they intend to extend your life.

reps

TABLE OF CONTENTS

Preface

The Priceless Treasure   9
perhaps a core of religions and philosophies

About Tahiti   13
where primitive and civilized pretend to meet

Pillow Education in Rural Japan   17
children teaching parents

Writing with Water   22
calligraphy as therapy

Sweet Sour Saliva to Young   26
a Chinese method of long life

Two Eyes in Fiji   30
health plus

Sweet Samoans   35
how to be happy though grown up

How to Solve the World Problem   38
unpossessed

Wandering Japan Alps: 40
Come at Once any Alps are in us

The Prophet of Tabuse   44
shows a way to shake well

Tea Communion and the Beat Generation   49
smooth move

Listening to Gagaku with My Eyes 52
music to purify with

Exercise Yes Exercise No 55
animal knowledge

Going to Hell with a Buddhist Nun 59
in the dark

How to Smoke Roses 61
yoga

Blind Amma-san 63
accordingly

Letter from Buckminster Fuller 65
our foremost designer of futures

Noh as Revelation 67
centering into glory

Norway Wedding 69
northernly

School for Receiving 71
a perfect position

School for Love 74
the sustaining consideration

School for See 76
a reason for images

School for Smell 79
beneficial fragrance

School for Touch 82
adventuring

School for Feel 85
and you are you

How to Die 89
without troubling

My Four Wives 92
from sun

Rejuvenation and Long Life 95
can be yours now through a secret 5,000 years old

■ **8** ■

THE PRICELESS TREASURE

perhaps a core of religions and philosophies

*When the Japanese invaded Hongkong,
Chang Pei Lin served as one of the native
policemen and so saved many Chinese lives.
Speaking both languages, he knew the
Japanese did not understand the Chinese
nor could his people comprehend their
invaders.
Yet every woman understands every man.*

A man of China, Chang Pei Lin, gives the way to me. Let me give it to you.

Sit comfortably alert all through (if it takes an hour or a day to do).

Let eyes close softly.

Listen in heart.

Listen: Openly attentive. In heart: Your felt center, core, stem.

As you listen, seeing quiets.

Thinking stills.

Positive passive meet. This instant you lighten. In some unexpected surprising way you return to your original nature.

What may you hear? No sound. Sound sharper than in ears. The unheard breath of life.

Even these take you from the point. The point: *Listen.*

Formerly every teaching shared this immediate way. In China it was simply Listen. In Japan, an almost silent chant into heart. In Persia, *hoo* outbreathed over heart. In the Himalayas, the sound of sound.

Of it, faiths have been voiced and the way obscured (by interpretations). Ritual, prayer, meditation, intellection have missed it.

It may not be received from books (from seeing and thinking). Complicating the doing, you miss it.

Listen.

When we met, Chang poured the treasure over me: "Resolve your life. How else will you stop thinking?" By thinking, he meant our habit of breaking in pieces our one life.

The same day I tried it, sunk into listening. My personal world (of troublings) vanished at once. Another time such listening brought a thunderous lightning flash, cleansing and healing. He told me the doing makes for well being. To begin with, it erases mental agitations like letters on a blackboard.

Perhaps aliving comes faster than thinking. Perhaps continual divisive thinking has us overpositive. Then any natural act recharges us.

When standing, he loosed himself until he seemed made of rags. He showed me how to close eyes as if I never had done so. And to listen toward center.

"We may have 3,000 worlds to wander as humans," he said (as an inner-space man). "Even if you live 1,000 years you must sometime die. Disengage your lightness any time."

Is there a lightness we are of more than light we see, as the inner light of flowers? It was like telling a weed to return to seed.

Yes, if we are of dust, we are of light. Yes, if we are aware, others of other densities may be more aware. If man's progress (out) takes him to far stars, he only may find himself there, the outside of himself. He has yet to find himself all here.

Himself: Just as he is, cosmos-intermeshed, limited and so unlimited. All here: When unseparate all are here.

Probably plants, fish, turtles, birds are better at listening than we with our constructed confusion. We go out too much or get put out. We are too little thankful. The baby has more to loose let than we.

Listening potentials. It heals subjective and objective sickness.

Conscious thinking may be energy-draining. Listening is energy-gaining. It stops starts something with clearest focus and least effort.

The wild deer listens, sees-smells-feels alerts.

You may have been too educatively frightened to try such a prime faculty. Or too busy. Or preoccupied. If science-bent, you may cancel out this you as a dead bird (instead of a winging singing). These days we have no announced way to inwardness so richly enjoyed by woman and child (and before them saturate in grasses and trees).

It is easier than you think. You are the way.

What about the listener? This listener provides our problem. He is having a go-go nightmare.

He is me.

I cut the one power and beauty into mine and yours. I go out. So I may return (to the life of spontaneity).

Aren't we already returned? Sigh, shiver, cry, fragrance tell us so. One who says: I, me, we, never parts from great nature. He only thinks, dreams, pretends to.

Then fortunately, he laughs.

This considers listening in heart. Ordinary listening starts in heart before we know it. We are the miracle. Ordinary seeing mirrors a total field. We shape things. We say "I see, I hear" since light and sound as us are one. Put another way, our infinitely possible life presses through special sensings. It pours through and all sensings open at once.

How to open?

Suppose (lightly) eyes mirror includingly, as they do. Suppose (gently) listening to silent music, wrapt, in. As we listen, we are being listened. We do it and the whole magnificence does it as us.

Then the childfreshing.

■ ll ■

root still —
buds
will come

ABOUT TAHITI

where primitive and civilized pretend to meet

Why go anywhere?
Aren't we already here?
Mind moves. It's hot. Take off your
clothes, skin, bones. Take off through
universe freely.

If we who are in this world such a short time have opinions about it, why not this after a few weeks in Tahiti?

The English have something the Indians lack (integrity), the Indians have something Americans lack (cosmosity), Americans have something everyone lacks (instrumentation). Scandinavians have something Italians lack (stolidity), Italians have something Scotch lack (song), Chinese have something the Burmese lack (intensity), the French have something the Japanese lack (love). Japanese have something the Australians lack (gentility), Mexicans have something New Zealanders lack (gaiety), the Fijians and Africans have something everyone except the Chinese lack (super-vitality).

This brings us to the Tahitians (ease).

From the porch of the old Stuart Hotel in Papeete, the only city of Tahiti, you can count 40 boats moored along the shore, boats of all sizes from an ocean liner to tiny sailboats hardly wider than Volkswagens, from Canada, Africa, California.

A stream of bicycles, motor bikes, some cars and many walkers, often barefoot, pass like a parade. The reef stretches far out where the waves are breaking white, and at sunset people just look and look.

Cheeks are kissed in greeting, first one then the other. The quiet-voiced French manage the island.

Like tropical Ceylon but with a milder climate, like Hawaii but still with a native population. Tahiti may be a last paradise.

A Tahitian lives in a thatched house whose roof and sides are the woven leaves of the coconut tree leaning above it. It was like this before he began to build with board sides and a hot corrugated iron roof.

He sits and looks, listens to the sharp-voiced birds. When hungry he walks over and picks up a mango, a coconut, a pineapple, a banana, or goes for a very successful fishing.

His life of ease, friendliness, and love sometimes slips into one of drink, indulgence, and disease. He is married but probably not to the one he is living with. The many children, the smaller ones often naked, move freely from home to home, loved but never possessed. Ownership is unnecessary. Dogs do not bark at you as in Japan where they snarl, guarding their owner's possessions. A restaurant across from the bank in Papeete feeds dogs and cats as well as humans.

Mountains, boats, and sea take on a dreamlike quality in the rain.

We go around (a world) to see a face. Each Tahitian face is friendly. Down a crowded street in Rangoon I once passed a ragged man with such a sunlit smile he still sticks in my eyes. In Burma too the women are free.

Along the Ganges a yellow-robed ascetic had the face of Jesus. I first saw the Sufi, Inayat Khan, in a Los Angeles hotel far far in himself listening while a woman sang atrociously.

In Tahiti anyone likes nothing better than to stop and speak with you.

When you breathe this flowered air, drink the cascading water, eat the fruits and just sleep, you too become sweet.

The women wish to be taken (what glances!) and by force.

A gal passes carrying a sack so large she has to hold it over her back with both hands. Her eyes open wide beckoning, but not to carry the sack.

Older women tend to be coconut-fat. One told me she had high blood pressure but she owned a hotel. Patting her strong hard shoulders, I asked her to stand feet straight ahead and apart and swing loosely from side to side, head too. She was bird-quick to get the idea, being a natural relaxer, and blood came back into her lips, her shoulders softened, and she felt much better. A half hour later she came back asking, "What was that motion you showed me?"

Yesterday or what was said or done then is forgotten today. Crimes are lightly punished or forgiven.

Get on a motor scooter and go slowly the 50 miles around the island over a smooth road mostly without hills. You pass hundreds of Tahitian homes with folks sitting in doorways waiting for you to come, talk, eat, and sleep with them.

Flowers line the roadside. There Gauguin lived between 1896 and 1950. You see his bright colors everywhere, in sky, greens, sea, colors that are ever changing. If you will abolish shoes and clothes you too may regain your loving mood.

Probably this is not for you as a tourist who must hurry, plan, shop, rasp. You are put in a costly hotel a few blocks back from the sea breeze where you swelter and sweat. Pores open, rain from within, as you begin to be a portion of a consuming nature. Rather than face the experience you quickly leave for "home."

"Tell me about Tahiti," someone asks. You do so, having seen it from without. Never, never look within. If you do, you might lose money, wife, newspaper, and be forgotten as some roadside flower. After your return you may describe the place as one of dingy Chinese shops, bars, foreigners trying to find themselves with native women, dirty restaurants, careless drivers, near squalor, drunkenness.

Take your choice, paradise or degeneration. Each person's world is his own intent.

The crunch of countless head-size, fist-size stones roaring louder than the waves as they grind themselves into black sand.

Does the black sand feel black to my feet? In this wind both coconut and newspaper civilizations are blown away like flies.

A girl prodded me from behind by mistake in the movie, then put her hand most lovingly on my shoulder to make amends. Touch here is always loving. But they don't approve of mouth kissing I am told. Passing a woman

■ 15 ■

in the dark she touches my face gently. I lift an arm to brush her hand aside. Who fears, not she.

Ugly missionaries taught the women to cover their breasts. By the way, what day of what year is it? Hawaiians dance with a free flow of arms and a loose pelvis. So do Tahitians, only the pelvis moves much faster. These dances no longer are sacred, with meaning. Even so, bare feet are better than high heels and bare bodies preferable to multi-storied cement prison cells called apartments in Hawaii.

At a branch in the road I meet an American in shorts, resident here 23 years. He tells me of a Frenchman's book giving a concentration for soul healing: first on blackness, then over a period of days the blackness turning to a brilliant light. But this is the story of 24 hours in Tahiti. Poor man, whose dark and light are isolated from nature!

Over the cliff, far down the green forest, the stream of my urine was never clearer.
The three most beautiful women I ever have seen:
* A Yogini (female Yogin) sitting in the white dust of a Karachi, India railroad station, firm-breasted, wasp-waist, naked except for some big beads, two Yogins straight and lithe, one on either side of her, and what a queenly self-respecting expression!
*A Japanese girl, Fukue-san, my secretary, without face-consciousness or makeup, modest with a skill of entering into another's mind and being there as if she were you.
*A Tahitian young woman, tall, thin, high cheekbones with a touch of Chinese blood, a face without a line in it glowing as if some kind of flower, revealing an unearthly earthly beauty of nature that should be all mankind's, dare we recognize it.

Suppose you find a Tahitian beauty and live with her. She cannot converse with you except in one way even after she learns your language. The chasm between man and nature so easily bridged by the native is magnified by modern man because he doesn't wish to give up fire and the wheel. No one does.

May he learn to be natural again? Has this learning to do with romanticism of the South Seas or with his own nature?

People of the world are trying for it with travel, tours, trailers, caravans, sports, play. But, wherever we happen to be, we enter our nature directly.

Tahitians are without jealousy. They need not think. Neither here do I.

PILLOW EDUCATION IN RURAL JAPAN

children teaching parents

These children are solving their own problems, even producing them to solve them, with child deliquency unknown.

How do you solve your problems?

In growing up, as much as we do grow up mentally, each of us has personal difficulties and social problems in relation with those about us.

In rural Japan a group of children are meeting their difficulties in a splendid way and even teaching their parents how to do so.

They gather together weekly in a small building near Himeji in Hyogo Prefecture, communally built and owned by their parents, mostly farmers.

Here they practice this method of education along with some arts and crafts and a body-motion calligraphy done with large brushes and water on newspapers. Their meetings do not interfere with but help their regular school work.

They are using a method of thinking for themselves that works. If someone has done a child an injustice, if his feelings have been hurt, if he is in pain, if his or her father is quarreling—anything becomes the subject of the study. They have no name for it, but since it is done with a pillow it might be called pillow education.

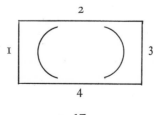

A pillow has four sides and a middle. A problem has four approaches and a middle.

For example: A child is slow in his school work. It is his turn to show the group how he is thinking through this situation. He sits before the pillow, placing his hand at 1.

"Suppose I can't think quickly," he says. "If I place here at 1 'I can't think quickly,' then this may change at some time.

"Here at 2," he continues, placing his hand in the 2 position, "is the place where I can think quickly and easily."

In doing this the child has objectified a handicap. He takes a look at it instead of letting it corrode inside. He also has imagined the possibility of his difficulty resolving.

He continues: "If 1 is where I can't think quickly and 2 is the place where I can, then I will say that here, 3, is a situation where I can think both slowly and quickly, where 1 and 2 are together."

This third step (the 3 place on the pillow) merges the opposites 1 and 2, just as 2 reverses the problem originally placed at 1. This is education in action done by the individual for himself or herself. There are as many girls as boys in the group.

It is a fact that most adults can only think to 2: white 1, black 2; right 1, wrong 2. "If I am right as I am, 1, you are wrong, 2." Entire lives are lived with this kind of thinking. Such dichotomy, either-or, right-wrong, often results in private and public unresolved differences.

When we consider the millions of dead in recent wars from a few leaders not being able to think beyond 2, we see how urgently such education is needed.

"You say you are right, father, and our neighbor is wrong," the child tells his father who is in a property dispute. "But may there not also be a place where you are wrong and he is right. And both of you may be wrong and both right. And at still another place, 4, all this may be forgotten."

"What are you talking about?" asks the father.

The child gets out a pillow. In a few weeks the father, considerably interested, has visited the school.

Such sharp thinking came from a very young child. He had a method of thinking. If he finds no difficulty to solve for himself during the week, he begins looking for one. When called on in class, he doesn't like to be without a subject he has worked on.

The child reasons not in numbers but in a relational sequence of four steps: wrong, 1; right, 2; both wrong and right, 3; and neither wrong nor right, 4. He does this as if walking a 4-step figure with his hand and with his mind.

In conclusion each child summarizes his presentation by cupping his hands in the middle of the pillow ( ), affirming an unnamed center from which 1, 2, 3, 4 emerge. It is as if he holds the complete problem in his own hands at the center of the pillow.

He then places the hand at 4, 3, 2, 1 and concludes by saying, "All these are gloriously affirmed," or "Each of these steps is good."

It is a tremendous relief to the child to be able to reverse his thinking and not be continually held in one viewpoint. In such kind of problem-solving, "nothing is the matter," their mentor says. A rebellious child joining the others invariably becomes gentle in a few weeks.

Susumu Ijiri, the originator of the teaching, an entirely humble man, says that he teaches nothing, that he is only a pupil of our unspoken source of being. The deep respect he has for life, along with his son Masuro, his wife, and many friends, reflects in the attitude of the children. Masuro Ijiri directs the school, or sometimes a wife of some farmer does.

The number of students has grown from 3 to more than 30. The meetings are a happy time. Students are entirely unhesitant about making personal problems public.

All kinds of subjects come before the pillow: Hunger and not hungry, beauty and ugliness, environment and mood, a bucket of water and a sea of water, blood of Orientals and blood of Occidentals, after my death the world will be and will not be—anything that troubles or concerns the child.

Even the pillow itself is treated as a subject: "When 1, I first heard of this study, I grasped it easily. But 2, since I understand it, it never finishes in me."

Another child offers:

"Here 1, I will say that American culture surpasses Japanese culture. But here 2, I will say Japanese culture surpasses American culture. And here 3, I will say that both American culture surpassing Japanese and Japanese culture surpassing American are correct.

And here 4, Actually neither does any such surpassing.

Moreover since all these spring from center ( ), in such a view 4, 3, 2, 1, each is fully affirmed by me."

The children do not count with numbers but use names for the positions, HI RI HO KEN (TEN), a Japanese five-steps-into-universal-harmony of unknown origin. It may derive from the Chinese Book of Changes. Susumu Ijiri says he developed pillow education (named by Reps) from an intensive study of Borobudur symbology. He has thoroughly explored this edifice in Java.

"The center of the pillow (we first used a small rug) represents our originative harmony from which changing conditions stem," he says. "I may say this but the children *feel, experience, and apply* it. Looking for difficulties to resolve should help them in many ways as they grow older. It has helped us who are older. We try not to place ourselves in a dominant assertive 1 position but rather to let, we don't know, 1, turn into something we do know, 2."

When a girl is troubled by a coming grade-school examination she really is troubled. Facing this fact, she is better able to handle it. She knows how to place it, to reverse it, to include it, and to surpass it as best she can. She has a method of thinking.

However effective the method and happy the results, their teacher continually de-emphasizes its importance before the center ( ). The central receptive attitude he feels is the needed ingredient.

In this he reflects the sincere reverence for life common among the farmers of Japan. Simple wood shrines, some not much larger than a bird's nest, stand by the farms where the Giver of life is respected in passing with a silent bow, a spring of green.

The books say these are Shinto shrines of many gods, but the farmers themselves never dismiss their relation-with-universe with such an intellectual shrug. Their feeling parallels the practice of the presence of God by the Quakers. With the children it is all practice.

The student's building is inadequate. They are poor. They share clothes and food with those still poorer. But they have declined publicity for the group, thinking it might only bring more problems. "Someone else must tell others about our method, we don't know how," they say. They are too busy using it in their own lives.

Have you something troubling you? Have you a pillow? If so, you may join these children in their wide way of thinking. It is not easy to translate the feeling of one person into the language of another and to convey in words the sensible delight of gentle hands on a pillow showing parents how to think.

open, head
open, heart
open
bones

WRITING WITH WATER

calligraphy as therapy

Give a child a crayon and it will start to
draw on wall or paper. Behold, a line!

The line comes before meaning. Each mark
is fresh. No life movement is repeated.
This is why calligraphy is therapy
and calligraphers live long lives in
the Orient. The vibration through their
writings has been found to be the same
before and after they leave this earth,
according to Occidental instrumental tests.

Write largely on wall or into air
to feel better.
Baby sees tree, points, "Tree!" Later
a language about it follows. "This is a tree."
But not in Chinese or Japanese.

Their language made of picture-words shows

Tree.

Blossom.

Dog.

Run.

They often draw such pictures, finger
on palm, to explain what they mean, a kind of
picture thinking. They sentence themselves less.

Almost everyone has seen Chinese calligraphy, characters originally picture-drawings written with a brush dipped in rubbed black ink. In China and in Japan they are considered a primary form of art. Simply by looking into them, one perceives the person of the one who drew them much as a hand-writing expert does from ordinary script.

Picture then 25 or 30 boys and girls from 4 to 25 years of age seated on tatami in a small house they and their parents built together, a number of open newspapers before each one, a large ink brush and bowl of water to the right. They are members of a group in rural Japan near Himeji City in Hyogo. Many of the parents are farmers.

After sitting completely still for some time, a youth lifts the brush, dips it carefully in water, and draws a single line on the paper. The brush is then put down and the person rests. Or, an entire calligraphic character may be drawn with sweeping lines.

This is done in silence. Perhaps one of the instructors may show how a letter is made, even taking the brush-hand of a child in his or her own and helping with a first letter. After any assistance, the pupil bows silently in appreciation.

"Draw this line," they have been told previously, "only as you feel it to be the most worthwhile act of your life."

"Draw it with your breath."

"The line flows from brush with outbreath, although variations of it change as breath changes."

"Let the line come from and go on to infinity off the tip of the brush."

"It is less drawn than experienced."

"Not only brush, hand, arm, but heart and mind draw it." In Japanese, one word, *kokoro,* stands for both heart and mind.

"Your line is an everywhere point and curve."

"The line, not aiming at perfection, never ends."

"Let center draw through you."

Do this brush stroke over and over as the youth does, each time newly.

After 100 or 1,000 such strokes done with utmost consideration, a great harmony of motion sings through you. You feel more than elated. Your mind has entered the line and universe.

■ 23 ■

How may this come about simply by writing with water on newspaper by people who are too poor to buy unprinted paper and inks? When we do something repeatedly, our nerves-muscles-ligaments learn how to do it more easily. This happens in riding a bicycle, in chopping wood, in singing a note, or whatever our tasks. The organism gets the idea and takes over. We may call it the subconscious mind. Until we educate this mind, we have only learned superficially. To live what we know, we must do so with our entire being. This being thrives in harmony of motion, in composure, in intelligent guidance.

Practice is a way. Breath is a way. Poise is a way. After these are gone beyond, we experience our true nature, more than something called this or that mind.

The drawing is not called *Shuji*, calligraphy, but *O-Shuji*, the drawing of God, if you wish to so translate deepest honor. It is a way of life.

Unruly pupils who come soon become cooperative. A teacher sits beside one in turmoil, simply sits, and then shows how to move brush with breath. Even in a few minutes the pupil composes within. No attention is given to changing an individual, yet immediate changes for the better are observed in students.

If you are inclined to rush or fume O-Shuji soon relieves unguided impulses. No part of arm is tensed. Should you feel it while it is moving, it would be soft and pliable. The brush is drawn over the paper, never pushed.

The shape of the character drawn does not matter. It is the one drawing who matters. Almost everywhere these days we find the drawing or product valued and the producer neglected. Things have become of more value than their makers.

In writing with water, a child's health often improves. It is said that even if you think of your favorite line while ailing, you feel better. This could be so, as tensions are relieved with visualized movements.

The writing proceeds in silence. After this weekly hour the tools are laid away, the newspapers dried. No laughing or joking occurs at this time, for managing oneself is more than play. With such practice one easily becomes an artist in everyday living.

To avoid any weariness, the character drawn is changed, yet only a single line is needed to discover *who* is doing what.

Sometimes what you draw surprises you. "Did I do this?" you may ask. "I could not do so. It must be *center*."

There is a center of you, a center everywhere in and through you. Once touched, life freshens. It may be touched in a brush stroke or in whatever we are doing.

So if we get some newspapers, brush and water, and try this, what happens?

We miss the presence of and respect for a teacher and through the teacher for ourself. We give up before 1,000 of 10,000 strokes. We lack the confidence of a group. Our breath habits tighten. We think of instead of surpassing ourself.

And doing so we lose our greatest treasure—the opening of our unwritten everywhere *center*.

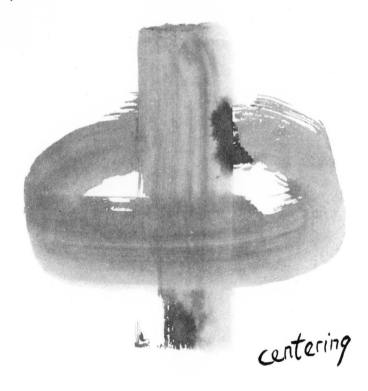

centering

SWEET SOUR SALIVA TO YOUNG

a Chinese method of long life

*There really is a Bao Che Man at
508 Chatham Road, Kowloon, Hongkong—
much respected by his people for his
skill in the Chinese healing arts.
He sends his sea-shell powder to
friends over the world. He does not have
a long silver beard.*

Among the Chinese it is well known that the ground powder of sea pearl keeps people from growing old.

Actors and actresses take it, many rich persons. It is too costly for the common people who often see their noted ones looking as if they were 30 at 60. They attribute it at least in part to this medicine.

Bao Che Man was a Chinese physician young in years but wise in learning. Using four methods he became so skilled that he found no patients he could not help. The four methods: to look at the patient, to smell him, to speak with him, to know his rhythm in relation with nature's.

With eyes closed and three fingers pressed firmly on a wrist, Dr. Bao received his information. To explain the technique of judging rhythms of nervestream and bloodstream would take a book. After a penetrating diagnosis he would order appropriate herbal preparations usually to be taken as black or brown teas.

One day a woman named Lee Shih came to him. She asked him to make her younger, telling him what he already knew, that the sea-pearl powder would do this for her but that she had no money to buy it.

"I cannot afford to give it to you," he said, "and you cannot buy it. So how shall I help you?"

Lee Shih explained, "When the sea shell opens in its natural environment, sometimes a small bit of sand falls into it, and as it closes it cannot get this irritant out. So it puts a saliva coating around the sand that eventually becomes the pearl. The longer in the making, the larger the pearl."

"We know this," said the physician.

"But what is not known," continued Lee Shih, "is that the inside of the sea shell, shining as the pearl, is made of the same saliva. How can such a soft creature make such a hard shell? It does, with its sweet sour juices. Its shell made from the same saliva is very cheap, in fact thrown away. If this were known, everyone in China could have such an elixir!"

Dr. Bao looked at her in astonishment. His life intent was to help his people.

"Why does it have such a good effect?" she asked and then answered. "We have two skins, one outside and one within to be cleansed. The powder clinging to our inside skin slowly returns to saliva and antiseptizes the convolutions where food poisons may lodge, so giving us a younger looking skin and delaying our aging. Or our internal rhythms are as sea and shell. Anyway, give me this powder. It matters little if it comes from shell or pearl."

Dr. Bao made it himself from gathered sea shells, mixing it with suitable herbal remedies into a small pellet in the Chinese manner. He gave it to Lee Shih regularly. A curious effect set in. She seemed to grow both younger and older. "Can it be that my sea-shell powder is only partly as effective as the costly sea pearl?" he asked her.

"Not at all," said Lee Shih. "Do we not see persons making themselves younger and older every day, even momentarily, younger with a mood of joy, older with stiffening concerns and worry? If I may grow both younger and older I am delighted, for then I will stay the same age."

"But I will become older," replied the physician, "and finally you will not have me to give you the potion, and it may not have an equal effect from another."

"True," she replied. "We give not only with our shells but with our heart."

He continued giving her the elixir for one, two, ten years. She kept about the same age, he grew older with a long silvery beard.

"How foolish I was," he thought, "not to have someone give it to me too."

Just then Lee Shih appeared looking as if she had made a discovery. "Let me be your physician," she told him.

"And how shall you treat me?"

"Of course with the sea-shell powder and herbs."

"But I am wondering how much the effect may be in my mind."

"I am mind," Lee Shih answered. "Did I not choose to give me the elixir? Did I not ask and receive your help? Need my mind be apart from that soft and hard, from sea and earth and saliva?"

"You speak as if you were one of our immortals disguised as a lovely woman," he commented.

"I am disguised as myself," said Lee Shih, "and so are you. This is why we need medicines. Each thinks itself to be itself or himself or herself."

"Well, isn't it?" asked the doctor.

"It is and it is more, for we are made of the great fullness."

Lee Shih gave him the compound. He too began to seem younger as well as older. He could find nothing in the old books to explain this.

"What is this mind?" he asked Lee Shih one day.

"Ah, that you may not know, good physician," she said, "until you discover it in your heart."

"What do you mean by that?"

"Men die and women age," she explained, "thinking they are men and women. As you put mind or attention *in heart,* both what we call mind and heart dissolve in lightness. Just as the dissolving of the sea shell purifies our blood, so dissolving the mind in heart purifies our human being."

"The ancient philosophy may be true but how do I *do* it?"

"Easily," said Lee Shin. "Touch the top of your mouth with your tongue, sit most easily with eye closed, and *listen in your heart.*"

"What do I listen to?"

"Sounds, tones, words of guidance may or may not come. But thinking and troubling vanish *as you listen.* Believe it or not, our heart's light transforms our worlds."

They live in Hong Kong, which is China, today. Their friends and relatives have aged and passed away. Times have changed but they live on, explaining to no one, for who would believe such a thing possible?

If you go there, become sick, call for a Chinese physician, and happen to get Dr. Bao, you will be lucky indeed.

I take his compound. I do not know what herbs he gives me or what proportion sea shell or pearl. I do not need to know. All I need is to feel his three fingers firmly pressing into my wrist, his eyes closed, his heart listening.

Do not write me for his address. It would be too lonely if you outlived your loved ones unless you could dissolve mind and heart in light. Then, being your own best medicine, you would need no sea-pearl powder.

Stamped
on buttocks:
100 year Free Lease
must be re-turned

TWO EYES IN FIJI

health plus

How to shrink a head in Fiji style.

Empty the skull of its contents including eyes
and tongue. Then stuff the entire head and
nostrils with flax.

At the neck, where the head has been severed
from the body, draw the skin together like the mouth
of a bottle but leave an opening large enough
to insert the hand.

Wrap the head in a large number of green leaves
and hang it over a fire until it is well steamed.
Then take the leaves away and hang it again to dry
in the smoke. This causes the flesh to become
tough and hard. Hair and teeth will be preserved
and the tattooing on the face will be as clear as
when the person was headed.
Among the Maoris of New Zealand such heads had a
trade value. Dried heads were sometimes sold
in advance of the killing.

Our head shrinks slightly in sleep and as
blood pressures are reduced. A person who has some
command over his organic function can shrink or
enlarge his head at will.

The idea of concealing the body with clothes
and leaving the head exposed may be dangerous.
It accentuates its value as a sign of how we are
invisibly.

■ 30 ■

Just before waking, I sensed emerging from an insect world. May we pervade other life forms in our unconscious experience?

Fijians were considered cannibals 100 years ago because they ate sacrificial flesh as some Christians do today, drinking the blood (wine) and eating the flesh (bread) of the gentle Jesus.

It may have been the flesh of a succulent girl or a brave defender of another village absorbed by the victors. The sacrificed was clubbed unconscious, his head broken on a "phallic" stone, and he was laid in a leaf sandwich over hot coals, covered with earth and steam-cooked until well done. His flesh was not touched but partaken with wooden prongs (fashioned today by Indians for tourists' salad bowls).

The Fiji men were fierce fighters as men are likely to be. Even today two nations have performed ceremonies to sacrifice every human on earth.

Is the mind we call primitive and the mind we call conscious the same mind?

The more than 300 Fiji islands, many uninhabited, lie 1,100 miles north of New Zealand. Yes they do. Arriving in Fiji by jet plane, I was astonished to see and be seen by a Fiji man. He looked straight at and into me in a most comprehensive way. His thick bushy hair stuck out like electric bristles. He had large eyes, fine teeth, a magnificent torso, muscular arms and legs, and very big bare feet.

Each other Fijian, man or woman, looks into you. "Bula," hello, is all you need to get an instant "Bula" in response. Most Fijians speak excellent English, required in their schools.

Melanesians: (Negroid, Fiji) dark-skinned, fuzzy hair.

Polynesians: (Tahitians, Hawaiians) sunbrowned skin, smooth hair.

Europeans: white-skinned, wilted hair.

If you wish to make friends with an entire village and perhaps live there, buy a bundle of Kava root from a Chinese shop, walk into the village, and stand still. You will be seen from all sides and shortly welcomed in the chief's house as one bringing him the best possible present. The root shrub will be mixed with water and you will be served their Yangona or Kava drink. Enough of it with rhythmic hand-clapping will take you out of this world.

A village consists of any number of tall squarish houses with thick-hatched roofs, woven sides, and mat floors. Each is built to last about 15 years. Slant-

■ 31 ■

ing bamboo poles rise to the peak and support the thatch tied with decorative colored cords. The entire house is tied as a house should be.

You probably will see some old iron or wood beds to honor any possible foreign visitor. The Fijians prefer to sleep on the earth. A family and relatives live in one home. The toilet and cook-houses are separate smaller structures. Cooking was done in a large earth vessel with a rounded or pointed base, supported by four stones. Vegetables in it were steam-cooked, with a little water, the opening plugged with a grass lid. Unfortunately costly aluminum pots are often used now.

The abundant vegetables and roots in this hot green land together with fruits, coconuts, and fish comprise their adequate diet. Children born weak or twins were eliminated, inter-racial marriage forbidden, and a strong race bred. American soldiers worked with the athletic Fiji men during the last war.

Air was made of gasses and greens only a billion years ago. We have not always been air breathers.

Bones of animals on earth 175 million years ago have been found. Neolithic man has compressed 2,000 years of "progress" into the last 100. In the last 50 years man has come as far as in all known history.

"What is your philosophy?" I asked a big Fiji man. He didn't know what I was talking about. "What is your view of the world?" and "What do you think of the people of the world?" also drew blank responses. But when I said, "I feel a kind of life under a tree, its roots through earth, leaves in air," he responded tremendously. His philosophy, nature itself, he simply waited for me to come alive.

"Are you a cannibal?" I jokingly asked a girl standing on a rock near the sea, another girl hidden in the bushes near her. "If we were," she replied, "we already would have eaten you."

These people have the strongest hair and feet. We might well appoint them our titular kings, queens, presidents, officials.

Mynah—bulbul—turtle dove—kingfishers—sunbirds—parrots.

Their Kava ceremonies are drummed and danced. The war dance with clubs, spears, and vigorous movements might be cultivated by anyone as a health and fertility rite. They will gladly teach it to you. Unlike improvising jazz as forgotten incantation, the Fiji rhythm in music and motion repeats one basic theme with individual variants. As it continues it *intensifies* to the point of the spear until the "dancer" can't miss. His whole being goes into it until "death" is least possible, for he has come most aliving.

Firewalking, still done on one of the islands, over stones so hot that paper thrown on them instantly blazes, is performed after extended (heightened) incantations.

These people have a nature-given intuitive sense we have almost lost.

Not only do the dead move through the living and the living through the dead but man through nature.

The Fijian has a good time of it. He prefers human to machine ritual. It is possible for him to be "spirit"-invoked since we all are anyway and since he has no arbitrary fixed-feel limits. The lovely objects he makes and uses are not "art" but living symbols. He is far more symbol-conscious than we are.

In each village an older man or women acts as a healer. If you get stiff, swollen, or sick, you may be rubbed with coconut oil so strongly that you cannot help but recover.

Walai invited me to his home in a village near Korolevu. How royally loosely he walks! He is ready for necessary but never unnecessary work. He never hurries and looks on those who do as if they were not *present*.

His village lies on a wide grassy plain near the sea where on a reef he showed me the underwater wonder world of coral and fish. The six months from April on are the coolest months to be there.

Since a large house communally built by perhaps 100 persons may cost less than $500, perhaps a Fiji village for foreigners might adjoin his wherein, with a few added amenities such as screens, some of us might bridge primitive and trivialized existence. This might preclude you from being a tourist, although tourists might come and look at you. There are of course some expensive hotels serving as tourist traps for unhappy foreigners rushing through them, of which Korolevu is best.

Saimoni, who works in one of the hotels in Nadi, invited me to visit him. His quarters were one 12 × 12 room in an ugly cement building. As I entered I woke some of the four children almost naked on the bare floor. Two men were stretched out asleep in their work clothes, their pillows the only furnishings. Buxom women sat along the wall and so did we.

Two older men went outside to give us room. A thin one danced in the hallway. Other men came, one with a mandolin, and soon they were singing loudly. This singing goes on often all through the night.

Of course everyone secretly examined me, the foreigner, after shaking hands. Their welcome was sincere. A big fellow I sat next to never even looked at me but rather felt my presence clear through. He knew all about me—and my potential movement. Everyone in this near-squalor was happy but surely much less comfortable than in a village.

For fuzzy Fiji hair, rub hair with ground coral mixed with wet red clay, leave on overnight, wash off, and rub hair with oil of a berry of a certain tree and a little coconut oil. Wait.

It is said Fiji was ceded to Great Britain by its inhabitants. The English brought East Indians in to grow rice and sugar while the natives let grow bananas and coconuts for copra.

Fijians dislike the snobbery of both Indians and English, although what may seem snobbery may simply be lack of heart communication on the part of the English. Or, it may be the habit of get more, give less. In any event, self-determination is only a matter of time. Fijians say that if the English left, they would have the Indians out in a week. The Indians say that without their business acumen, the natives would return to primitive ways. We see between the Indians and people of Fiji the contrast between effete and primal cultures.

In his village the Fijian lives a communal cooperative life. His every decision is made by his chosen chief. He is not an individualist and is lost when he leaves his community.

Perhaps he has something to teach us individualists: how to live naturally in a garden of Eden. We need not go beyond our own back yard to do this, but why not to Fiji? If you do, meet the Fijian man as your equal if you dare. If you take pictures, let the children look in the picture box. It will delight them. Ask the wife about her home and family. She is better attuned than you with earth, sea, sky. At least she knows that every being is alive, including the dead.

SWEET SAMOANS

how to be happy though grown up

Rain bubbles
Somebody's troubles

In the woodland you press my hands.
Brown leaves
pressing on
wet brown leaves.
Here twist of tree and snake
are of one make.

The Samoan taxi driver in Honolulu sang softly along the ocean.

"Why are you folks so sweet-natured?" I asked him.

"We eat fish instead of meat. We gather poi wild. We have some fresh vegetables. We don't have to work for anyone. We never worry that we should be doing this or that. We are all like brothers and sisters. We can live on the milk and meat of those coconuts. We fish and swim and enjoy life. Why shouldn't we be happy?"

He was a smiling embodied antidote to the commercial world, kingly without coin, kindly without a trace of condemnation. We arrive at the simple home of Aivao Leota. Aivao is 80 and stronger than most men of 50, a Mormon missionary to Samoans and Hawaiians. Some white missionaries once came to his father's home. His father beat them so Aivao went off with them.

Although I was a total stranger, he was very happy to see me. "Now that we have met, we are one family," he told me and meant it. "Come and live with us." He knew that once persons touch hands, invisible threads weave between them. He gave me a Samoan uatogi, a twelve-pronged war stick. He gave me an ipu, a coconut cup. He would have woven a tapa cloth for raiment had I asked him, but these could have sufficed for at least a year.

I sat with the stick at my right hand, the cup in my left, green and yellow leaves dancing in my eyes, the sea breeze blowing through me. As a Samoan, had my ancestors sailed westward as American Indians or eastward as Egyptians and Hindus? Both are told of in legends, but this was a long time ago.

Aivao also offered me a wife.

In Samoa one of the neighboring kings once asked him, "What are you smelling around here for? Get out. We don't want you Mormons. Get out."

"But I am not white, I am Samoan like you," he replied.

"Get out, get out," exclaimed the king petulantly.

"You haven't long to live," he told the ruler, "or your wife either."

In a few days the king died. His wife followed him. This had the effect of increasing Mormon membership considerably. Of course Aivao could see that petulance and exclusion, traits so foreign to Samoans, do not make for longevity and said so.

Another time Aivao fell from the top of a coconut tree, crushing his leg and back. He was nursed alternately by Samoan-Mormons and Samoan-Samoans. Then he was sent to Hawaii. Children, grandchildren, and Mormons in multiples surround him now.

"We live for the dead," he told me. "Around each of us are a hundred recently dead as well as many more. By praying for them we help them. By baptizing my wife I seal her to me now and hereafter. Once when I was in bed with my second wife, my first wife who had passed on came to us very lovely. I baptized her and now I am sealed to both of them."

It is only white-skinned persons who believe they are alive when they are alive and dead when they die. Hindus, Japanese, Chinese, Samoans, Tahitians, and old Hawaiians know the specific spirit of life never ends any more than do coconut trees. They know *consciousness* inhabits form.

Our head can't figure this out. If he lives anywhere, the devil lives in the head. Someone lives in our heart, so well hidden there hardly anyone can find him.

Yet almost every Samoan has found this living *being* in heart. This may be why he is so sweet.

Fish oracle

IF Fish
turns
south

Let's go
south

HOW TO SOLVE THE
WORLD PROBLEM

unpossessed

*What right have you to impose
your ideas on me?*
    *The right implied when I listen,
absorbed in them.*

*What right have I to impose
my poem on you?*
    *You already are making yours
before you start to see or say.
This is the best poem.*

The Shinkyo Community has done it.

Over 22 years ago a group of farmers five miles from Hibara, Uda-gun, Nara Prefecture, Japan joined houses and land and labor to start a new way of life. They shared everything except toothbrushes and wives. At first they grew rice and other agricultural products; now they are famous for their excellent tatami, floor mats, and have more orders than they can fill.

All their shared profits went to improving their living and continue to do so. They reside in splendid quarters, daytime at work, but kings and queens or butterflies after 5 p.m. when they throw their work clothes into washing machines and enjoy their large O-furo, hot bath, together. Then, fine food and entertainment.

"Shinkyo" means "mind sphere." They have only natural body consciousness and are free of the sense of private possession. They accept no gift unless each of them can share it. Every month they move from room to room or house to house, so they need not be possessed even by a room.

When one of their number leaves the community, as he or she is most free to do at any time, the competitive struggle for existence seems to bore him. So he returns.

Mantaro Ozaki, Ritaro Ozaki, Kyujiro Yamanaka, Masakazu Mitani, Yoshi Sugahara, who are the founders, were jailed as suspected Communists during the war and were later released. When official Communist representatives solicited their membership, Ozaki said, "You solicit us because we are successful and respected. Our idea has already absorbed yours. We are farmers with a shared cooperative ideal, that is all. We need no ideology. We have freed the human mind by channeling man's aggressive urge and woman's possessive urge. We are happy, and we are growing. But we are not trying to reform the world—only ourselves."

Ozaki, while highly philosophical and intuitively religious, is a practical Japanese farmer who well knows the fallacy of trying to think beyond oneself to doing compulsive good to others. He knows how to mind his own business and how to manage the subtle monster, mind. He and his associates have solved the world problem.

Poem
OF
unsaid
words

WANDERING JAPAN ALPS: COME AT ONCE

any Alps are in us

It's Spring.

It's Spring.
Sing.
Breathe this almost-mile-high air. Sip this tonic water. Wander the greened paths. Come at once.

Wherever I go in these Alps the mountains fall on me. The farther away they are, the closer they appear. Oriental artists who have painted them have been accused of lacking perspective but this is how they look. An act of light makes far near and near far.

One inn advertises: 15 rooms, can sleep 100.

It is customary to put many persons in one room when necessary. Sometimes the tatami is so crowded that even the floor telephone must be put outside. A lot of laughter, then all is still. At dawn the sleepers are off to the peaks.

Boxes, little boxes called cameras hang on shoulders. Almost everyone carries a box to take dead pictures of living scenes, later to lose them in some desk drawer.

Here comes a Japanese professor, an electrical engineer. I tell him, "Man projects his wiring systems out of his own nerve patterns."

"Cybernetics?" he asks.

"No." I say. "As soon as you intellectualize you lose your joy."

He understands this at once, for Japanese are masters of mood living.

O-furo, the hot soaking bath, heats the inner man until the heart speeds the circulation and sluggish aches dissolve.

Eight of us are soaking in o-furo. I make a shogi-playing friend in the hot water.

On the way to Myojin Lake we meet a young couple. He is lithe, empty-handed, the happiest man—over nothing. She lugs their huge pack on her back, pleased to do so. It is not work to her. Somehow the woman always carries the burden.

Mt. Otaki, Yake, Nishi-Hotaka, Yari, Okuhotaka, Maehotaka, Mt. Myojin—the hikers weighted with their packs climb them all. Sometimes alone, often in couples, most often in groups, up and down they go and I don't hear a radio, see little smoking, smell no sweat. Japanese perspire but unlike some other races do not smell. Their minds are clean.

They stop breathing at night, closing windows tight. They are right. A sleeping bear breathes into his own fur. A bird breathes into the lungs. It also rests. But if possible it is better not to breathe another's air.

I meet a thin man and his wife, both in street shoes. He speaks of his travels over Europe and Hawaii. We talk and I enjoy his joy. So does his wife. When he smiles she smiles. When he laughs she laughs. Her whole mind is in his.

A Japanese woman knows how to be a wife. She keeps in total agreement with her man and she does so for a lifetime. Or shall we say she used to before she learned how to chew gum, paint her face, pull out eyebrows. Before she kept her mind in her man. Now she loses it in her mirror.

A good swordsman goes with the movements of his opponent. He takes over the other's motions and kills him or spares him.

Japanese go with, rather than against. Our world is learning—to go with.

The art of going with is called "Tai Chi" in China where I try to study it with a great teacher. He puts his fingers lightly on the neck of his opponent, goes with his movements, and without apparent effort tosses him about at will. He might kill him in a moment. He never tires for he does not use his own energy.

Lao Tze philosophized this non-resistant way in "Tao Teh Ching," a book often translated. You can't even climb a mountain if you don't go with it.

Most scalers of heights wear thick-soled boots. They chomp along like deep sea divers with their feet weighted.

I prefer jikatabi, earth shoes of the farmer that have the big toe separate from the others so that the foot articulates. You can jump from rock to rock like a goat in them because the feet take hold. If you fasten your thumb to your hand with bands and use your hand as a club you will know what you are doing to your feet in Western-style shoes. Nerves from feet stretch through body. If you bind these nerves, don't you bind yourself?

When sleeping in a small inn a huge storm comes. Rain falls in torrents. Lights go out. Wind howls. Blackness. Trees fall. What a symphony!

In the morning the trail is broken by two new rivers.

A man in hip boots carries us across on his back, a kind of boney palanquin.

The widening streams rush to sea. The electric air cleans. Leaves sprinkle the paths. The loam is sweet and so are we.

"Where are you going today?" the maid always asks me.

Finally I tire of being forced to decide what I don't know and reply, "I am going to the benjo (toilet)."

"Would you like to go through the inland sea with me?" I ask her.
She thinks about this.

Then I show her three stones placed before the tokonoma as my stone garden. "There is the inland sea."

How she laughs!

Japanese make the loveliest movies and the best of these have samurai in them. I stop a fellow on the road and ask him, "I want to meet a samurai. Where are they?"

In the Peacock Princess movie the shogun's daughter comes to marry the Prince. When they first dine alone, she throws him through the shoji doors into the yard.

"He tried to lick my lips with his like an animal." she complains to her lady-in-waiting.

It's cold. I put on tanzen and my long underwear for lunch.

Rice sprinkled with black goma and brown rice huskings.

Onions and green peppers cooked in soya oil.

Miso-shiru soup with a little salt and lots of wakame.

Shiso-no-mi, seed of shiso.

An apple.

Tea brewed with mountain water in a China, not an aluminum, pot.

And a spoonful of mountain honey.

When calling for a yutampo, a hot water bottle, in my bed, I ask the maid if she is a yutampo too.

She puzzles, blushes, then laughs.

Soon the entire inn is laughing about it. Everyone from owner to maid works and laughs together.

I am shown a postcard of a tiny village in the mountains.

"Let's go here."

Not to know where one is going the day or hour before is best. You take the cement skyscraper, give me the low wood building. You wear the necktie, give me the old shirt. You worry over the news, give me the glory of these mountains where the people are red-cheeked, where the fisherman blends into the stream, woven into nature as each of us must be someday.

Standing in the forest and slowly turning, I seem to hear a silent growing, feel a presence, and am healed.

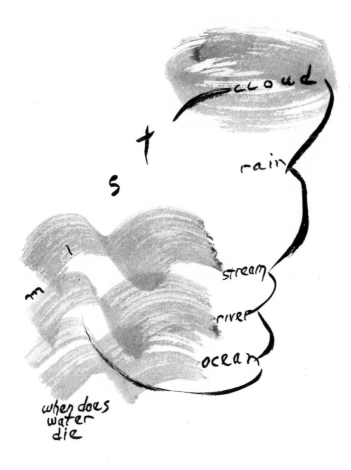

THE PROPHET OF TABUSE

shows a way to shake well

Like people, religions organize and ossify,
lose poetic quality. Any belief that condemns another
is itself condemned. To elevate oneself with words
and worst of all with religious words is the
ultimate cupidity. "My religion is better than
yours and if you disagree you go to hell." Thus
organized religion has become ludicrous. But
before the religious constructions, what wondrous
stirrings come from the human heart.

In 1944 the male deity, Kotai-Jin, and the female deity, Amaterasu, entered
the form of Sayo Kitamura and there became a trinity. Some think of deity
as spirit, but Japanese understand it as a specific spirit of guidance.

Sayo Kitamura was born Jan. 1, 1900 in Tabuse village, the fourth daughter in a family of nine children. In 1920 she was married to Kitamura as his
sixth bride, five previously driven away by his widowed mother who had
used them during the work season and then dismissed them to save the expense of feeding them. Sayo was worked so hard she had little time for food
or sleep but refused to desert her husband, eventually winning the approval
of his cruel mother.

In 1944 the voice from her abdomen spoke to her saying, "Osayo, polish
your soul, polish your soul." Confused by this voice that continued per-
sistently, she tried to be rid of it, even considering suicide. The guidance it
gave however was always right. Identifying itself by several names, it finally
told Sayo that here was no local, but the supreme deity come on earth
again to help humanity and that Sayo had been chosen as a means.

So it is narrated in a book, *The Prophet of Tabuse,* a translation into English of a longer Japanese work (*Tensho-Kotai-jingy-Kyo,* Tabuse, Yamaguchi Pref. Japan).

It tells about a simple farmer woman, subject to severe disciplines, becoming a prophet. Japanese began to call her Ogamisama, the godly one, and she is known today also as Odoru Kamisama, the dancing goddess, and Ikigamisama, living goddess.

The teaching

Ogamisama teaches that we are responsible inspirited beings and that while here on earth our finer substance or soul should be polished. The polishing is to be done with prayer, with the cultivation of non-ego, and sometimes with an ecstasy dance to dissolve self-love and wishing to be loved.

Science today and religions of past centuries agree that we are more invisible than visible. Our everyday conduct shows us as feeling beings rather than solid packages. We tangle in regrets, wants, dislikes, attachments. Unable to resolve our life and negative to the influences of others, present or absent, we become subject to adversities.

Ogamisama has a dynamic alternative. She says these negatives which make for weakness, and self destruction may be released. Her positive practices are for this purpose.

The prayer

Her prayer, while deriving from an older Oriental form, is unlike what is generally known as prayer in the Occident. Ample precedent for it exists in ways variant from hers: Nichiren, 13th century: Namu-Kyoho-renge-kyo; Shin-shu, 13th century: Namu-Amida-Butsu; Chinese Wei Dynasty, 220–265 A.D.: Nan-Wu-Ah-Mi-T'O-Fu; earlier Indian practices.

It is as if we were a bottle that needed vigorous shaking. To shake the bottle from within:

Close or soften eyes from seeing things,

Press middle of palms together

and let them vibrate or shake while singing or chanting Na-myo-ho-ren-ge-kyo softly or strongly, keeping attention behind center of eyebrows. Do this morning and night for 5 minutes or more.

Observing devotees of this teaching in Hawaii and Japan, I note these possible good effects from the sustained practice that may account in part for its widespread use:

Closed eyes with pressed palms center body and mind. Resonance, singing, with rhythmic motion refreshes.

Internal organs, glands, and tissues are vibrated head to feet (felt while doing it lying prone). Cerebrospinal fluid, lymph, blood, regenerative juices are circulated and rejuvenation begins.

Stiffness, aches and pains lessen. Sediments and sentiments are loosened. Tubes and pores opened, we are more apperceptive. It helps assimilation, gets us out of inertia, electrifies dull areas.

Inner originated (not done to us by another), it strengthens and positivizes.

It stops short-circuiting thinking and worrying. It exercises without violence. As a whole act it restores our wholeness, our well being.

It frees brooding spirits bound in us by immediate and distant ancestral tendencies assumed in negative states. Almost everyone is a walking hotel for these ghosts or subconscious tendencies registering unhappily as nerve-muscle congestions.

It gradually shifts attention from out or in to up, from self to soul or whole. With inner music (ours) and inner rhythm (ours) we refine.

It cultivates gentleness and exaltation. We are inspirited.

Some such results may be probable as the "prayer" is entered into wholly, with sound welling from below, with a sincere heart.

Muga, or the non-ego condition, naturally follows. Mu (no), ga (ego), spiritual ecstasy, stepping up of consciousness, is less translatable in English than in us.

The active prayer is followed by a quiet period alone or with others of muga cultivation, asking forgiveness for egotistic inclinations. This selfless orientation immediately relieves subjective and objective inharmony.

It is said that Ogamisama can see in a person tendencies implanted through generations. People of many races refer to these as spirits. When English-translated, we call them subconscious influences. However named, it is these deep trends we must release, and the more inspirited we are, the more we may "spiritually" free.

Inspirited: the opposite of spiritistic, innerly positive rather than negative, invested with inner power and glory. Spiritistic: ghostly.

Shake
the trunk
not the
branches

reps

The dance devotees over Japan, Hawaii, and U.S.A. meet weekly in their homes, pray and sometimes dance together.

Close eyes
and let yourself move
as you feel
to improvised singing.

Anyone can do this. To see hundreds of persons young and old dancing so simply, freeing themselves of human troublings, brings tears to one's eyes.

Such muga in motion is unlike dancing that overexerts and fatigues, that requires skill and training, that few can do, and that young and old do not do together. It feels like being rocked in a mother's arms and such good good feeling may continue into the next day. It is what dance may be.

It should be more enjoyed than explained. If we know why we do something, we say we are intelligent. Yet our knowing only surfaces our wisdom of being and can separate us from it. A greater wisdom is woven in our cells.

As we are humble about our assumed knowing, as we *play* we know, great nature becomes more friend, less enemy. Japanese, though often over-earnest, are ready players, singers, and dancers. Their religions tend to be enjoyable rather than threatening.

Ogamisama has patterned much of her teaching after the Tenrikyo faith which has many more "followers", whose beloved founder was also a woman who taught movement with chanting. Of the many modern religions in Japan, these two try to sing and move it.

TEA COMMUNION AND THE BEAT GENERATION

smooth move

*Ever since writing this poem, I
have been unsuccessfully trying to live it.*

> *Drinking a bowl of*
>
> > *green tea*
>
> *I stopped*
>
> > *the war.*

*A Chinese friend writes: "Don't worry the war of the worlds because your
poem already stopped it.
Each poem gives the world one year happy.
Please make more and stop the war forever if you
make thousands."*

Tea communion:
An old Japanese custom of serving powdered green tea with slow motion
to open the mind.

Beat generation:
Younger generation over the world addicted to jazz rhythms as a means
of shaking loose the constructed pretenses of civilization. Beat means beati-
tude or bliss, not beat up.

Believe it or not, these two aren't so far apart. Both are after God.

Now why bring God in here? Because God or Kamisama or Allah or
Amida are just names for a wholifying experience man has gone into for
centuries.

How do you wholify? Stop againsting. Stop fixating. Move. Swing.

Ah, but jazz gets going faster and faster. Not as smooth cool jive and not as tea communing, paced and slow.

Take your choice: fast or slow—but pace it, *even* it, and you wholify.

It's as simple as listening to music. You hear the beat, emphasis, breaks, but under them you feel the deep melodic you. It's like waves and sea, foam and the very first low down current of life.

Jazz is for the world. Proof: The young of many languages accept it as a common language.

No matter how much you celebrate, you don't know much until you feel freeing—and this feel is available, fresh from Africa, in spontaneous *evened* rhythm.

Perhaps some unknown African humming into the world is in-balancing all the top-sitters, culturists, politicians, priests, and pompous killers. Black is night. Night, the unknown. What we know is only for a day anyway and the truths of this year are the untruths of the next.

How can tea and jazz meet—the quiet server of green liquid in slow motion and the smooth in-toner for joy?

An airplane drops into an Amazon jungle. The native Indians don't know what to do with the thing. Neither do we know what to do with our fine instrument. We do know it feels better as it slows. We are more than a stick or stone. We're a confluence of rivers, a compact of airy currents, a transmitter of invisible Light.

In slowing, we become more aware through our channeling. By grace, not by trying force. By joy. Or even in utmost despair. Chinese called it the heavenly heart in the center of the head, the Light of our world.

A young woman once served me tea at Ura-Senke in Kyoto so quietly, so simply. She keyed into pure mind. Such unforgetting moments are what we live for. We don't just live for any moment. The more such moments, the more we live, even if our time on earth hardly is longer than that of an insect.

Something refreshing happens in tea communion. The server serves. The one who sips the green receives. Well, that's it, *receives*.

Something happens in smooth cool jive. One sends, the other receives. We receive from our fount of being, not just from a tea bowl or a horn. Then, from them too.

So it happens—something opens in our middle and maybe tea did it and maybe music did it and maybe you do it with your unexpected glance.

Need you be detailed in the opposite: the poor rich sitting staring into their moving boxes, the vacationists roaming with their little picture-boxes, the merchants arranging boxes on shelves, the collegians with boxes fastened in their heads, the protesters breaking boxes?

World (no larger than a peanut) had two kinds of humans: those who move and those who don't. Those who move, accord. Those who stiffen, fight against the moving heart, nerves, tendrils.

Of the movers there are two kinds: Those who break motion and those who move smooth.

Slow motion opens the mind. Smooth motion opens the heart. Slow smooth motion turns on the *inexplicable delight*.

So when we sip tea we're in communion, so when we jive we're alive.

I see again your faint secret smile. We're all in this together, in this wondrous happening, energies undissipated, in slow continuing motion.

receiving

reps

LISTENING TO GAGAKU
WITH MY EYES

music to purify with

> *The instant we are conscious we are.*
> *My greatest mistake: I have seen, have said,*
> *have known—in seeing blind to beauty,*
> *in saying deaf to melody, in knowing closed*
> *to love.*
> *Whenever I correct another, my bliss cuts*
> *off. Then all I impart is imperfection.*
> *If the loving kindness of folks were added up,*
> *even the clouds could not contain it.*

Ga (gracious) and gaku (music), ancient Japanese court music, is something to see with one's ears and hear with eyes.

It is more. It is Shinto magic. Today even the performers do not comprehend it. They just do it—in resplendent costumes, with stately movements, with dignity. They show us how to respect movement itself.

From the first slow whine of a wind instrument with its reeds pointed heavenward, then the flute sound, the boom of a large drum decorated with a mandala design, a metal gong, then some large seed-shaped instruments, a koto joins in—twangs, whines, clinks, beats—slow sustained rhythm like a procession marching in the skies.

I have seen this music and dance at Ise, wandered around and heard it from outside in back where the sacred white horse bows his head to the ground, hypnotized by the sounds. These inevitable slow sounds and movements were meant to lift us out of our nonsensical goings-on into a living peace.

■ 52 ■

The musicians sit with fabulous costumes, phallic headpieces, and wrinkled interesting faces, pictures of rocks and spirits.

The dancers enter with still more fabulous robes, lavender over red before a gold screen or a temple when performed out of doors. With wands in right hands, they stamp, swing, bow, squat, whirl, and even jump towards center and the four quarters of universe in acts of purification.

How can such get-ups, such whining tones purify universe? Very easily. The universe is in us. As we subject ourselves to guide motions in rhythm we become purified—even in seeing them.

What does purified mean? When the blood pulse is put in rhythm, the heart exuberates. Our heart is crying day and night for the luxury of natural rhythm. It never gets it from us, hard-driven by goings and gettings and doings. As a result we die without once tasting the grandeur we really are and that Gagaku shows.

If we appreciated the worth of this court music, we would hold it sacred or at least valuable enough to teach in schools and to enjoy as movement in itself. We are the court. We are the Emperor of our domain. Before and within us this dance occurs—and in the white horse.

Now men will dance. Now girls more gracefully. Now a dragon appears in a silvery mask and long nose. Now four beings issue, their faces hidden by flat clothmasks impressed with seed designs. After two hours of this, universe is so purified we are never again the same.

We go forth in a daze, released from petty tensions.

never never
sound
see
whisper
touch

much

refa

EXERCISE YES, EXERCISE NO

animal knowledge

The time may come soon when there are
no books but words and pictures on a screen
enacted for and through us. Learning may
become doing.

Exercise yes exercise no. Animals never exercise. They keep moving. They move and rest move and rest move and rest. They go around naked, eat unfired food, when wild, sleep outdoors. They never die. They return to animal.

Man never dies. He experiences something he names death, but he cannot conceive I am not.

By airplane two hours north of Stockholm in Sweden and an hour of driving into the forest brings me to the finest athletic training establishment perhaps in the world, the only one with spring moss.

Here at Valadalen, the name of a no-town, I meet Gosta Olander, world-famous for having trained more champion athletes than anyone else. He has spent 35 years in the building of these dwellings, athletic fields, skating rinks, ski jump, and a fine mountain hotel with the healthiest young patrons. I ask him his secret. He does not say. He shows me.

He takes me to an 800-meter gray sand beach edging a lake. You run a few miles in this soft sand to strengthen your feet and legs. Then you jog over to the spring moss and run on it barefooted. Each step springs you up, so soft and pillowy is the turf. It helps inject a flexive response through your musculature. It is like running on a mattress—only better.

Then you continue running on one of the many narrow mountain paths made by the Lapps with their reindeer herds, narrow so you run in a straight line up and downhill with stamina. Next you return to the spring moss for release.

It takes only two or three weeks of this for you to become a runner. You take a plunge in the cold pool and are ready for superb Swedish food. What buttermilk and applesauce!

You are doing all this at an altitude of 1,900 feet which produces more red blood cells immediately. In the pure mountain air, in an athlete's environment of no smoking, no drinking, no indulging, no idle talk, no cars, no sidewalks, no stores, and everyone with one intent.

Next you study the animals in a large zoo who teach you movement. The Himalayan bears show you how to move from center. The foxes, alertness; the wolverines, tirelessness; the deer, sensitivity; the flamingos, how to step; the crows, observation. No animals is so foolish as to define such qualities. Animal lives them as they live him. The ego is man's invention.

You study the Lapps in wigwam houses with turf sides and boughs for floor, men strong as forest trees, always outdoors.

Nature is speaking Olander's secret. No wonder all manner of athletes are learning from him. The air is charged with win. What is the secret?

Keep moving. Come out of doors. Learn from the animals. Go to bed with the birds. Get into the game of life. Eat live foods to build live cells. Welcome rain, thank sun, keep supple, sweet, move.

The strength, endurance, and speed Olander evokes in others are of nature. He only channels the big message into the champions, merely human champions winning at artificed games and remembering it the rest of their lives. But they get a rich reward. They live longer and better and cleaner for having drawn from nature, their nature.

Come in the batsdu, the Finnish sauna, where in the hot dry rooms your billion pores let go and out come the poisons and you feel fresher for a week. When you are pouring sweat, jump into the cold pool, in winter into the snow.

Three miles up that mountain is a lake full of fish. Run there. Spring. Save *your* life. All you have to do is to take to the forest, forget style and the paraphenalia of anti-you. All you have to do is to keep flexive, supple. Move smooth. Move and rest. Move all through. When resting really rest through every cell. Don't listen to others, don't be restless for amusements.

And when you move don't tighten your neck. Loosen those wrists. Don't make faces. Run ahead of yourself. Loosen that neck.

It's late morning, 5 a.m. The big bear opens one eye and looks at me. He uncurls, gives a tremendous yawn, curls up again, breathes a long out-breath into his fur and goes to sleep. The best sleep is after waking. The best waking is early. There's something in the air. The owl as large as a small barrel opens an unblinking eye. He sees everything he needs to see.

What is our mother nature but this shrub, this weed, this you *in relation* to this me, in infinite surprise relations. Pardon these stiff words for the adventure.

You can't run in heels, in high heels, You really can't. Here young women are as athletically inclined as men. What good is a construction that can't run? You can't be sick and run.

Run is only to run, 10 more steps each day. It costs nothing. To ever be sick is expensive business.

Heart is the mover. Whatever we think as mind only surfaces heart power. Animals move *with* heart. We are animals too, sense-crippled but cunning.

A man does what he must. Olander was born to teach athletes, to bridge man and nature uniquely. But how about us?

among reeds
weeds
each is
the other

GOING TO HELL WITH A BUDDHIST NUN

in the dark

*When we see someone we like we are
in heaven. When we see someone we
dislike we are in hell.*

She followed me down narrow stairs into a dark room. Placing my hand on the smooth wall, she pushed me on. Soon I was in complete darkness blacker than night. On I walked, my right hand on the wall, the nun behind me. At last we came to sheer nothingness. The wall ended. I was in hell.

I discovered a turning and continued to follow, on past two more turns. My hand struck a large metal lock and key. This was a sign that I would live long enough to unlock life's secret.

After the lock we came to the last corner and turned again. We had completed the square under the Buddha image of Fushimi's temple, and with her I emerged from what they happily call hell.

This old lovely temple is of the Jodo faith. Jodo-shu practices chanting as a direct way into enlightenment.

If you chant the sound *namu-amida-bu* your worries soon disappear. Your cells begin to resonate and come more alive. Chanting you feel good. Then you are good. No one who sings wishes to harm another.

Chion-in temple, of which Fushimi's is a branch, supported 95 nuns; now there are only 25. Yet they need only one like Teramori Kyosan or Tessho Kondo or Fushimi to justify nunneries. Such beings are more than nuns; they are radiantly happy humans.

Teramori at 74 is more dynamic than most women of 30. She has health and strength any youngster might envy. It is her way of life that gives it. Try it.

Sit erectly on the tatami, your legs folded under. Palms touching, with arms away from torso, to free breath and heart, quietly chant *namu-amida-bu* three times, bowing on the third. Your head touches the mat, hands opening to each side but arms not resting on the mat. Continue to do this 10 times, 30 chants in all with 10 bows. Do this twice daily.

Through tonality, the focus, the motions, your whole being tingles. A kind of electricity comes through, and you feel right. Worries leave you because worries dislike sounds and bows. Simple food nourishes you thoroughly. Your mind clears. How good to be alive!

Naturally you are delighted and thankful to Buddha (if you are a Buddhist) that this is happening to you. Other sounds or chants will also give you the experience.

Na-mu-a-mi-da-bu, na-mu-a-mi-da-bu, na-mu-a-mi-da-bu—and bow! Without years of recondite study, even a week of this practice will have you alert and alight. How the faces of these nuns glow! They are living in the shining instant.

Other women not nuns reading these words may go to Chion-in and see how they do it. Then as their hearts get stronger, muscles suppler, gestures quicker, rears and middles slimmer, friends—seeing the change—will want to begin chanting too.

Soon all the women of the world will be chanting and bowing and shining. This is sure to make the men happy. The women's minds, instead of being on men, sweets, clothes, possessions, will be free.

HOW TO SMOKE ROSES

yoga

*There is no harm in smoking. Our heart
is already on fire. The harm is in compulsive
smoking.*

*The hookah of India, when you suck the smoke
through water to cool, develops the lungs.
The tiny one-puff small pipes of Japan
are a ceremonial delight. The peace pipe
of American Indians was good smoking.*

*If the tobacco is sprayed with a habit-forming
drug without the smoker knowing it, he can't
stop the habit. He is compelled to smoke,
a drug addict.*

*Facing this problem I yelled loudly
"Stop! Stop!"*

"Stop what?" my undermind asked.

*"Stop SMOKING." I scared it and have had no
desire ever to smoke since.*

If you ask a Japanese "What does this sentence mean?" THE ROSE IS
RED, he probably will draw his breath in through his mouth politely and
feel roseness and redness.

If you ask an American, he will say, "That is a simple statement."

The Japanese feels. The American thinks. Both are right generally speaking, but how different! To feel directly makes a natural artist. To think directly makes a good technician.

The Japanese is so feelingful he is quick to adopt foreign ways when he chooses. He has been accused of being imitative when he is sublimely flexible. You have only to walk down the street of any village to see every few steps examples of his original handicrafts.

By feeling, one may escape the newspaper-radio-television unease afflicting millions of earth inhabitants. Man is most joyous when originating, and direct feeling always is original.

By thinking, one may avoid emotional involvements, traps for infants.

Feeling unifies, thinking divides. Feeling takes in, includes. Thinking evaluates objectively.

The excessive smoking of Americans probably is due to an unconscious wish for relaxation—to be had by drawing breath in through the mouth. No cigarette is needed to do this. Just by breathing in this manner one can avoid the expense and systemic pollution of a chemicalized weed.

In ancient Yoga the in-breath through the mouth was known to be a stimulant to beauty. The reverse of this breath, in-breath through nose and outbreath through mouth, gives health and strength as every singer knows.

The rose is red is not the point. Artist or technician is not the point. Japanese or American is not the point. The point is: What am I doing to myself with my breathing habits? Have I direction over this finest instrument or am I dulling its possibilities, repeating myself, playing the same tune over my brain-tracks, a slave of habits?

As an artist may I think more clearly, as technician may I feel more dearly by becoming aware of the rhythm of breath? Breath is more than air through a nose. It moves as pulse through heart, impulse through nerves, as life through cells, and it is sense as consciousness in our roseness and redness.

BLIND AMMA-SAN

accordingly

We are mostly blind. Our sensings
specifically limit us.
Otherwise we would see and be everything.
We are slowly unfolding this everything sense.

In the incredibly beautiful surroundings of Yataya Inn in Tatayama I was shown into exquisite living quarters. The clean tatami mats underfoot, walls of white, soft-gray sliding doors, ceilings of fine wood with silver and closely edged bamboo, the low tables, the tokonoma containing its single scroll and a flower beside it reassured me. The scroll's colorful long-beaked bird perched on a tall weed with withered leaves.

When arriving at a Japanese inn, you are given tea and a cake, then a yukata or loose robe to be comfortable in as you go to and from your bath.

Japanese are extremely clean people. Contrariwise the Eskimos tan their furs, their clothes that keep them from freezing, with urine. When they gather in a hot room, the aroma is indescribable. They are the only people who willingly wet their pants.

The mineral bath in a pool large enough for swimming, an outdoor garden pool where later young ladies disported themselves beneath my window, the delicious meal served with each food artfully placed on its unique dish, all put me in a pleasant mood.

I asked for an Amma-san, a Japanese man or woman, young or old, who presses each square inch of your body until you feel entirely renewed. It would be an insult to call this pressing and squeezing massage. It might be considered as internal exercise or a kind of deep ironing.

Each Amma has his or her own technique, and while a head-to-foot routine is the rule, none are ever the same. Motoko-san, for example, kneels on you and works on your back with her knees, a variation of the Hindu foot-walking method. A man in Mishima wrestles your body, quickly breaking every rigidity free. Some persons are done-in for days afterwards from so quickly becoming flexible against their will.

You also may try moxa, the burning of little herbal cones on certain areas of your body. Or acupuncture, the insertion of a needle through your skin until it touches a nerve and stops your pain at once.

I lay down in my yukata and she began pressing me: shoulder, arm, hand, fingers—then the other side—then slowly down the back. An hour went by. She depended on her feeling more than Amma-sans who can see. Occasionally her sensitive forehead wrinkled as if some part of me was not circulating as it should. Once my hand reached up and gently rubbed *her* forehead smooth again.

She walked down the stairs alone, as if seeing with her feet.

LETTER FROM BUCKMINSTER FULLER

our foremost designer of futures

*While we are traveling from place to
place or from room to room we receive
impressions.*

*We also give them. When walking down a road
we radiate impressions. Animals know this well.*

*So travel becomes our responsibility and
response-ability.*

*Buckminster Fuller travels in invisible
ideations, designing the nearly weightless
buildings of our near future. He shows us
structures a tenth the usual weight at a tenth
the cost, sometimes of a mesh so fine
as to be invisible yet housing an entire city.*

*Many records exist in India of persons flying
through the air. Patanjali specifies yoga
practices to make the body weightless.
As anti-gravity devices are rediscovered
we may swing in hammocks between the stars.*

*Yet to come into the presence of beings
we know not of, we shall travel in as well as
out and at will. Our human instrument
is for this discovery.*

Dear Sir or Madame:

I am a structural explorer, seeking for thinkable principles governing spontaneous associabilities and regenerative constellations invisibly embraced by nature and jealously guarded by her against ignorant inadvertancies of might-makes-right-vandals. I am excited and incited by progressively ephemeralizing, yet progressively augmented coherent capabilities of Lincoln's might giving rectitudinal integrities whose weightless intermesonic, internuclear, interatomic, intermolecular, intercellular, interstellar, intergalactic predictibility of positional-relationship functions, in universal dynamic reliability, are transcendentally exquisite to any intellectually sought, instrumentally informed, disclosure of fundamental error. I seek the only-universe-issued license to consciously participate in the local evolutionary formulations permitting, and enclosingly favoring, the nuances of evolution-generating advantage of both conscious and subconscious life growth, as the tendriling omni-frontier of becoming-intellect finitely comprehensive to its own principle of infinite rebirth. As such an explorer for local structural enclosures of life in universe, I frequently tune in the frequency modulatings of other explorers in the invisible economy of principles. Whenever it happens that I tune in the frequency of Reps, I am aware of his structural exploration in the patterning of structures of meaning itself. I receive his signals with almost instantaneous awareness of his deft realization of poetry's most-lucidity-with-least-word-work.

Everyone likes to hear nice things said about him.
Is this something nice Bucky says about Reps? I don't know.
But Bucky wrote this. Yes he did.
I read it. You read it. This makes three.
But $1 + 1 + 1$ *are not 3 but III.*
$0 + 0 = 0?$
No.
$0 + 0 = 00.$

NOH AS REVELATION

centering into glory

> *Poplars*
> *Look*
> *Gold*
> *is*
> *never*
> *old*

Noh gaku, Japanese Noh chanting and drama with vivid slow movements and brilliant costuming, gives us a glimpse into the enlightened mind. For "mind" to be "enlightened" our inner Light or *consciousness* should turn on.

To most persons even this statement about it seems absurd. Noh moves in a dark dream, trapped with vigorous tensions, imitative intonations, old stories, formal ways.

But look at it from the outside—as sheer sound, pure motion. Lo, you are in a new world. Sound springs from its seed, silence. Of the sounds of men, Noh most nearly suggests this silent singing presence.

What might be the secret of such in-guided motion?

Motion flows from center. From unmoving center of wheel many spokes ray forth. From unmoving center of me comes perfect function. This is to be *experienced,* more than said or read.

In center of feet, find foundation.
In center of back, find weightlessness.
In center of heart, bliss.
In center of head, directivity.
In center of seeing, stainless receptivity.
In center of sound, silent presence.

Anyone who cares to experiment with centering through balance, actual ease, nervemuscle ordering, weightlessness, will uncover at exact center indescribable refreshing.

Swinging completely eased eyes over the top of a pin, in-hearing tone, softening neck from top of head to body base while moving, moving smoothly, sitting in ease, lying in the sky—approach centering.

Touching center even for a second, one is as new all through. This is direct untellable truth.

The Christian conversion, the Buddhist wheel of life, the Hindu Infinity, the Chinese Tao, point to centering. Jesus in the Father, the Moslem in Allah, the one-pointed mind of Patanjali, the Chinese Golden Ball, mandalas of Tibet, Buddhist and Jain statues, show centering.

Our pulling stretching compensating body is trying to center. The thousand postures of yoga and the agitations of vocal and subvocal meanings, try for center. Center is everywhere happening. Yet the moments we are in balance are so brief, and we are so little aware of them, that centering seems to occur rarely, to few, by chance.

How shall we be free of inner conflicts until we cultivate freeing? On the stage of life our movement, so common and so continual, can mean more than relief from solidity, more than just getting about. In-sight, the core of sight, in-telling or self guidance, are here rather than out there somewhere.

In the center of a ricefield at Kawanishi village in Nara Prefecture, Japan a commemorative monument stands to Kanze (father and son), Noh originator. It is somewhat taller and wider than a shoji door.
It reads:

Thousands of practicings did not content him, a million moments of training and he was still unsatisfied.

Then one evening before dark suddenly a large fan floated softly from the sky to his stage, encouraging this pioneer of Noh to continue.

Persons devoted to this teaching place this tablet in tribute to the founder.

What is this but trying for untrying—for that moment when the very breath of heaven opens. Worth a lifetime of effort, it comes effortlessly, even as a great fan might open in revelation.

Noh plays used to be sacredly performed before Shinto shrines. What was and is the intent of this but to uncover the glory of our being?

NORWAY WEDDING

northernly

"Oh,
oh!"
may be the best poem of all.
It attests feel, spontaneity,
responsiveness and
vibrates through like a struck gong.

Rural Japan is a resplendent place to live in autumn, Hawaii in the winter, and the fjords of Norway in the spring—especially Sogn and Hardanger fjords, those long fingers of the sea with snow on high mountains and the green valleys and farms below. And the blossoms.

Yesterday, May 22, 1965, Nils Lothe and Anna Marie Samland were married at Utne, a tiny village on a tip of Hardanger fjord reached only by boat and one narrow road. The wedding party came in small cars in the late morning and parked down by the ferry in front of the 250-year-old Utne Hotel. They lined up in pairs wearing the colorful costumes of long ago. The procession began, led by a fiddler who played a lilting tune as the toastmaster walked beside him. The two fathers followed, then side by side the bridal couple with Nils on the right, then came the bridesmaids carrying the empty container for the crown, then in pairs many married couples, younger folks, and friends.

The bride-to-be wore the large gilt silver crown and had to stiffen her neck a bit to bear it. She was dressed in a red skirt, red jacket and embroidered bodice over a white blouse with many silver broaches, and low shoes.

Slowly, seriously, up the hill they went and into the large church with its interior of fine unpainted woods, the pews marked with wood carvings in the shape of crosses as spokes of a wheel, the sun. The church was full even to the organ loft.

The preacher dared to speak for some time as the couple sat facing him in straight-backed chairs. They rose then as he addressed them, pronouncing them man and wife and touching their foreheads to confirm it. Then they turned, the bride now to the right in the ascendent position, and walked slowly down the aisle, followed by the entire procession out under the trees and onto a green hillside to have pictures taken.

Then again led by the violinist and toastmaster, they walked slowly down the hill to the cars, followed by all the others, and drove off to a remote farmhouse for the celebration. There the bride was to change her costume and, relieved of the crown, put on the broad white starched headdress of the other women.

Before Norwegians became relatively rich it was a serious matter to be married. Not only to be married, but to live in Norway—a matter of survival. Wood had to be provided for warmth, and vegetables, cheese, and meats had to be obtained lest one went hungry. In the old days you made ropes of wood bark, spun your own wool, and knew the art of herbs.

The rigor of those times still showed in the faces of those in the procession. When you get to know them, the people of Norway are stone-strong, quiet as their trees, direct and kindly, and warm as their houses. Each one seems to be silently telling the story of the north.

May to September, the short summer, is soon over. The cold returns. Now it is light almost to midnight. I asked a barber in Stryn about divorces. "We had one of those once," he replied.

Nature is the adversary, almost never each other.

In the one-room store at Utne I bought oranges from Spain and apples from Australia. As our world is appling together perhaps we have something strong and steady to learn from those who live in the north way.

SCHOOL FOR RECEIVING

a perfect position

There must
be
something
green
inside
this
green
seed

Who doesn't wish to succeed, to be healthy and happy? If we could increase our well-being 1% or even 1/10th of 1% it would be worth while. This tells about a way to do so by taking a perfect position for a short time each day.

The idea of group man, economic or political man, stems from the individual man. When we look at the "individual" man, we come to you. Here is a way to amplify you.

Receive.

Sit, just sit, for five minutes each morning and night and receive.

This is so simple it may seem absurd. As you just sit, breath begins to flow evenly. Your self imposed tightnesses release. It is no small thing to do for yourself.

You might sit and plan or sit and worry. Instead, just sit and receive. Sooner or later waves of good feeling pour over you. Since it is too naïve to believe, try it. Be as a child again.

When sitting, feel as if silently singing. Let some *silent* sound sing in and out smoothly. Vowels are best for this though each of us probably has his or her own varying sound needs.

Japanese are especially trained in receiving. In their quiet politeness they show it in many ways. But they have forgotten the practice. They have lost it in ceremony and complexities.

Hindus, generally speaking, are trained from early childhood in receiving. Their gentleness and age-long use of prayer seem inborn. Yet they have obscured direct *receiving* with intricacies of thousands of religious procedures.

North Americans untrained in receiving overlook themselves before their conveniences. More truly speaking, instead of Japanese, Hindus, Americans, we are unique individuals.

Any idea comes to us by our willingness to receive it. The practice means (A) sitting in complete ease without moving, and (B) with a receptive attitude.

From whom do we receive? From our source of being—before names and forms, and then from all the wealth nature bestows.

We also receive in action:

Accepting a cup of tea is receiving.
Quiet composure in a crowd is receiving.
Willingness to help someone is receiving.
Remembering a parent or friend is receiving.
Joy in nature or in gardens is receiving.
Respect for the wisdom of someone is receiving.
Enjoying beauty in any form is receiving.
Music or song or dance is receiving.
We are receiving in innumerable ways to exist.

How do you double your success or skill? You practice doing so in some manner. An easiest way is first to put yourself in a state of innocence. In this condition possibilites multiply since you are starting from the beginning.

Receiving instant by instant, you should find energy, then health and originative ideas come without your doing anything about them. To place oneself in an inner unworrying willingness is like in drinking perfect being.

Each remembered teacher imparted receiving in some form. As you practice you understand the Amida Buddha figures of the Orient sitting and standing in a sublime peace.

The Nirvana or rising out of suffering that Gautama Buddha talked about becomes your experience. You appreciate the Japanese Shinto bow of immeasurable thankfulness for the great beneficence. It could be the Hindu or Christian bow. As you receive you realize what Jesus meant when he said, "Seek the brightness of Yahveh first and all else will follow." As you receive you know bow the Moslem feels who kneels to Allah, who is all, five times daily and why he is so refreshed.

Instead of drawing from outer sensings, our mind seems to tune in and draw from its roots perhaps as a flower from soil and sun. Our nature refines. Whether you receive little or much, do not miss this inpouring.

The daily practice replaces worry-hurry with a tincture of thankfulness and scheming with faith. It revivifies and restores and encourages and forgives. So it becomes the most valued space of our day or night.

Rhythm of sea and seasons moves as our breath. Rhythm of turning earth and sun moves as sea. To receive I turn towards my fount of being. Nothing may happen. I may only wait. I feel good doing so.

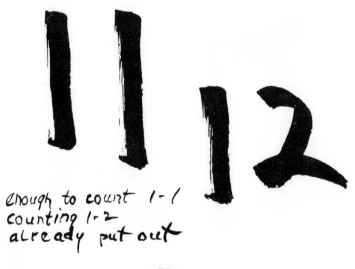

enough to count 1-1
counting 1-2
already put out

SCHOOL FOR LOVE

the sustaining consideration

> The snow
> is taking
> away
>   our
>   footsteps

Hypothesis: Love.

What we see and hear gets into us, Suppose it becomes images and imaginations. If we don't "suppose," if we tighten up on what we say, we cement ourself.

Images appear haphazardly in dreaming and in day-dreaming. Love is one of these. A big fine word in the Occident, "love" is rather looked down upon in the Orient as inferring individual overheating.

Suppose then we package images and imaginations. Can we release them? Can we take what we see and hear fresh, undefined with surprising possibilites, as if for the first time?

Of course. When we blink we relieve our eyes of image fixations. When we leave our tongue up against our mouthroof imaginations are released. This stops talk. It has been observed that throat muscles are talking subvocally much of the time until we quiet them.

As eyes blink as we willingly release staring, and as tongue lifts, we pause. This pause cleanses us of seeing strains and overtalk. If we continue pausing, trouble lines begin to leave our face.

If you stop visual fixing and imagining and pass your palms slowly over your face without touching it, you can suppose you are smoothing facial surfaces and you will be, since we tend to become as we image and imagine.

This subject is taboo. No one investigates the finest known instrument in universe, our own. We customarily overwork and overuse it, beat it up, wear it out without ever once observing ourselves instrumentally.

Where are we going in our rush for machinery to have living more convenient and to travel around the stars? We are going out and around. May there be another inner travel? May *who* be more important than what? May this *who* be the presence of love, not just the love we make and name but a brilliance including and sustaining us?
To touch this brilliance fills our hands with buds and flowers.

Well, I have marked some white paper with black words. You have "read" these words. On you go, on I go, but as we stop to consider whatever we are doing and *who* is doing, we are rather magically in another world, as if in opening our closed hands a new world appeared in them, as if a mother were holding her newborn child, as if everything were quite all right.
This considering, any considering, I call love.

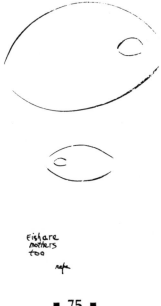

Fishare
mothers
too

SCHOOL FOR SEE

a reason for images

Fourteen yellow petals
blow
in the door

Flowers in your eyes
reveal more beauty
than those in the fields.

See a picture.

It may be, for example, flowers through a window or in a vase. Whatever we see makes a picture in our eyes that becomes an unseen portion of us. Our privilege is to let the image dissolve beautifully through us—as uncountable seeings do.

When we see something our eyes do not go out. Yet we say we see out there. If we think it is only out there, we miss something. As our attention goes out it makes a wide world. As it turns in it makes us sweet.

Graciously receiving and only receiving the flower picture, we feel rested, Letting it permeate us infuses us with a kind of ecstasy.

We begin with one picture. The moment our seeing softens, attention already has turned in. Our limiting has become an unlimiting experience.

Not only flowers but sunlight through us, breath of air, drink of cool water interpenetrate us.

Without resisting, our self-binding struggle for power of peace ends. Beauty begins.

As self-imposed strains of seeing are relieved we enjoy natural delight.

Let's pretend

this,
greengold

flower-field

in
our
eyes

reps

Weakness, troubling, illness can dissolve by un-seeing. It is incredibly easy.

In the place of beauty where one wall is inset in the Japanese home, we find a long hanging scroll and below it a flower grouping. Why do they give daily consideration to their companions of the fields? May the object we see be less important than the way we see it?

"I see maybe 10,000 pictures or images daily. You ask me to take one of them, a few flowers or a single flower, and look at it in a new way, rather to let it look through me and then to follow its image dissolving within like sugar in water.

"Is this possible to do? It happens but who knows where or how these light images become us?

"You tell me as soon as my seeing softens my attention already has turned in. You say this in itself brings delight.

"You feel that as the image merges in me and as I keep my attention on this dissolving as you call it, I come into an unlimiting instead of a fixing process. You suggest that in doing this experimentally I may be renewed or sweeter than before, stronger, perhaps healed.

"Please send me one flower to begin with."

SCHOOL FOR SMELL

beneficial fragrance

Never tell
a lie,
black butterfly

grasses

This subject is treated in old-style way, in sentence after sentence—subject-verb-object-period. Picture impacts are diluted.

Fragrance as a noun is unsmellable. If you fragrance something it feels less static than fragrance nouned.

We rise above subject-object-verb in the act of fragrancing or smelling leaf. To smell is not to dull.

" If you can't see you say you are blind. What do you call it when you can't smell? Smell-crippled?"

"I smell all right."

"Animals show us that our smell faculty is largely closed off. They are keener with it than we are."

"We get along all right without smelling so well."

"Yes, but may we smell too?"

A dog wanting vital information stops and sniffs it into his brain center. The sniff may be varied for verification. Then he or she knows and acts.

We inform more through our eyes. Might we also cultivate another neglected faculty of fragrance? What follows is five ways to do so.

When we intake an aroma (double-talk for when we smell) our nostrils open a little. This opens face slightly. Our face also opens inside (like an umbrella).

As our inner face lets go, anxiety lines begin to erase before they get imbedded in outer face. Thus smelling acts as a rejuvenant (medicine-elixir). Chewing honeycomb opens nostrils. Hungering opens nostrils. Delighting opens nostrils. You open nostrils.

Something else good happens as we appreciate fragrance.

Fine nerves in head vibrate (like harp strings). We may better anticipate the unexpected. We have ideas. We are using a skill instead of having it closed off in disuse (like an old closet).

In this way our friend the cow decides what grass is beneficially acid, a cat knows who has been in a room, a dog knows his master and welcomes him, a bloodhound follows dried particles of blood, a horse smells a bear miles away, a bear selects a root, a tiger senses man's courage or fear through the two-doored nose.

There also must be a yet finer smell sense than the informative one, something meshed with oxygen assimilation synchronous with breath.

Before the animal sniffs, it pauses. This pause also comes after in-breath. If we realize that we pause after a fragrancing, our breath slows. A habit of slowed consideration sets up so we live longer or at least wiser. An entire system of longevity later called yoga was evolved in the Himalayas on the principle of paused breath.

The pause has us keener feeling. It is built in. We do not have to do it. We only need realize the fragrance.

Probably we first smell what we say.

Whatever we say about someone (or ourself) registers in us. We hear it first and loudest.

We also breathe it. Our silent or spoken judgment falls upon our heart, our vital reproductive subconscious, with breath.

We are the producer and consumer of fragrances. We breathe ourself sweet.

In inner-face delight, in sharpened evaluations, in life extension by breath and with breathed judgments, we fragrance fragrances.

We simply wait and fragrancing comes in-as-through us. How we take it is our schooling. In "religious" orders of "prayer" in the Occident, and in "enlightenment" orders of "meditation" in the Orient, incense is burned so the quiet one may be lifted in awareness.

Such out-of-this-world moments each day make our work and play worthwhile.

Fragrancing, available for everyone before nouning, has these moments more frequent, easier and simpler to experience.

SCHOOL FOR TOUCH

Contortions of guts show in our face.
A desire or a fear registers in our guts.
This is why it is better to be honest.
It shows.

To get in touch, touch. In this touch you no longer are Japanese, American, African, male, female, young, old, but the living universe.

Suppose you see a sign SCHOOL FOR TOUCH and enter the garden to
ask what it's about.
I place a stone in your hand: "Feel this."
Then, a gnarled wood.
Then a rough-shaped bowl: "Touch, feel."
Then, some clay to knead.

As you start to talk I offer you a drink: "Touch this water in your mouth."
You do so.
"Let this bit of fruit touch you."

"What next? you ask.
"Nothing next. Just experience touch."
"But why?" you ask. "We are no longer infants."
I offer you a damp towel to refresh your face in.
"Touch refreshes."

All say you all Play ball
I say neither yes or No
I say Yes and No
I say "yes!"
I say "NO!"

Some pine needles brush your cheek. You slip off shoes and press loam underfoot, to smell flower fragrances.

"I still want to know why," you continue.

"No matter how far out we go with sense impressions, do we lose touch? In seeing, light touches us. In hearing, haven't we intertouch of sound vibrations?"

"Physical philosophy," you observe.

I answer, "You may say that touch is a physical phase of our personal feel but this only divides something with words. You may word it 'subjective' and 'objective' but touch comes before and through words."

"Child's play," you conclude.

"Why not? If we depreciate touch by calling it a mere sense, we miss its originative enjoyment. Then, so to speak, we are out of touch. If we call it a sin, as some religions do, we deny life."

I hand you a plastic bag filled with liquid, a small ball in center representing the human foetus in its amniotic fluid, protected from impacts yet responsive to the parental rhythm.

Before birth have we an inner knowing-rhythm-touch? During and after birth do we touch as our first communion and communication?

How a child appreciates a mother's touch, even the sound of her voice! A pat relieves an anxiety.

You step under the shade of a tree, then out into sunlight and into shade. I see you are experimenting with touch of dark and light.

We need shade, light, wind over our skin. We need to feel through innumerable pores. We think separatively. We touch wholly, all over us.

Sex localizes an area of touch. To get out of touch is not to feel.

"But we touch invisibly," you comment, as if, for you, seeing were apart from touching.

Touch, consideration, acts through our invisible-visible world. After all, no one ever has seen our face except from the outside. We feel face and much else.

If only we might put men intent on destroying one another into conscious touch!

Off you go, leaving me somehow in touch with you.

SCHOOL FOR FEEL

and you are you

Omori-san, Japanese inventor and manufacturer of automation machinery, tells me: "I used to work very hard thinking and planning. Now ideas come when I least expect them. If I need to know something I ask. As soon as I ask an answer comes. If it does not come it is not for me at this time. It is as if a life giver were speaking to me. This makes my work and life very easy."

Few persons in the world seem really unhappy. People get a lot of enjoyment from the simplest things.

Their joy is intrinsic, inborn. Yet everyone rushes here and there, when all the time they are happy as they are *because they feel.*

Clouds fold over a mountain. I point to them and say nothing. You agree. I sit at ease before the window.

You gently lift my arm away from my side and let it return.

"How does this feel?" you ask me.

"Like ice cream," I finally reply.

You wait.

"Unlike," you say quietly. "When it 'ice creams' the feel is gone. Keep in feel."

With this simple experiment you teach me more than many schools.

I know now when I am primal and when I am projecting into words or things.

the poems
are
for feel

thank you
for your
life

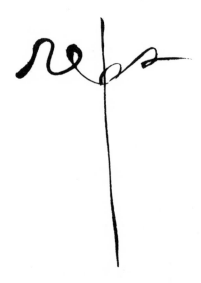

First the mountain feel, the elbow feel. Later a thousand interpretations. Poets break feel into words.

Painters try to squeeze feel onto canvas.

Sciences fix feel.

Religions extend feel.

This is too good to be true. It comes before "true."

In some schools where small children draw *as they feel,* where the teacher does not teach or change or praise or criticize, where whatever appears is good, the children grow strong in feel.

We never graduate from this school.

Some such indescribable subtle feel exists with happily married couples.

Somehow inventors, originators, discoverers, those thoroughly enjoying their work, feel.

Feel as emotionalizing, as reasoning, as intellectualizing, is obscured, hidden, as if it does not exist.

When we sleep deep we are honest in feel. When we wake we fight our way into our clothes, about 5 per cent feel, 95 per cent fizzle.

In feel we are in before—before ending, before beginning. In the feel of pain disappears. *In* birth pain where has the pain gone?

In feel I have yet to come to argument, disturbance, conclusion.

Raindrops in puddle, stones on river bank, leaf falling, eye of a frog, whatever appears is wondrous.

To see someone walk by, to hear a bird cry, dawn, dusk, black night, are for feel.

And you are *you.*

Rain

napo

HOW TO DIE

without troubling

Mighty men have marched with flowers.

When a woman would win a man she appears
to him as a flower. When he would win her
he gives her flowers and she at once gives
him her flowerself.

Ah, the soft shaking of flowers. Forgive
our loud voices, flowers, we were only
talking of fragrances.

Shall we be satisfied when we learn how to
behave as flowers, each on its own stem?
Who whispers me, "Invent the wheel?"

Asleep in a bed of flowers with strange
questionings excruciating pains shot through
me struggling in the dark as people
slashed about with knives. Exhausted I sank
into earth.

"Poor dear," someone shuddered, "you call
us flowers, not we. Long ago you left us
to become as you are, returned and left
uncounted times."

A humming revived me. At a moment between

sleep and wake I thought, "Now, only this
moment the will driving me to destruction
may be softened."

Man spreads his carnage for what? "That we
may grow in glory," a flower replies. Have we
been living to build a soil for flowers?

Even
crushed flowers
re-member

Even if we live longer than long we must sometime die. Though old age, poison from air-water-food, by accident, sometimes by violence we pass away. Consider then these 12 ways to die.

1. Dying is like falling asleep. We need not fear the experience yet often we do. Then die IN fear or IN pain. Fear and pain are of life. As we enter IN them they transform.
2. Each of us has some beloved image in heart, a father, mother, lover, friend, exemplar. Be with them in heart. This is a frequent way of departure.
3. Die in joy for being clear of a world of finite concerns, freed into our infinite being. The Burmese celebrate death in this manner.
4. Die singing. Whatever moves vibrates, shakes with life in a harmony as music. We listen to music IN. Listening IN heart to the silent sound we are is a splendid way to live or die.
5. If we would die well we gladly make room for others. As I consider another, the subject—I—disappears in the other. As I consider life, I may disappear into *life.*
6. Death comes to the closed self as a change of garments. Memory may end but not consciousness. Consciousness inheres in each being. Some may imagine becoming a bird or fish or another human in passing from this earth. We become who we are, consciousness in the arms of preconsciousness.
7. We are mostly invisible. We cannot see our will or desire or under-

skin processes. We see a light but not the electricity. In dying we simply return to our potential.

8. Before dying ask forgiveness of those you have killed and eaten, the animals. Ask forgiveness (in heart) of those you have thought, felt or acted against. This in itself softens our over-positive tendency.

We package positive-negative particles subject to our intent. Today the positive-receptive balance of nature on the surface of this small world has been disturbed by our thought and radio waves.

The Moslem bow in prayer, asking forgiveness of Allah, the one life, also softens the hard heart.

9. Some may say such ways of dying are ugly, too personal.

Seeing an object, it enters us in some mysterious way and we it. Subject-object are one. Frog waits eye-still for insect. Heron stands as a stone for fish. Watches. Suddenly. Bird in fish. Fish in bird. Is this life? Is this death?

Insect, frog, tree, mountain, man, clouds, sky appear and potential quite freely. What is there to trouble about?

10. We have faculties, the faculty of seeing, hearing, tasting, knowing. We also have the faculty of transforming. This faculty includes being born and passing away.

11. Our backbone may be as a kind of tube of awareness. At base, a blinding black seed light, at top of head a dazzling white light. Join these lights in heart in delight.

12. As we are breathed in the great rhythm fine muscles of our back release with inbreaths. As a cup we are filled with whatever we are choosing. As we are outbreathed our life energy circles over head and down into heart, showering cells with bliss. What we thought of as life is as death compared with this bliss.

MY FOUR WIVES

from sun

The spider spins her web, the fish twists,
the turtle cries raucously in love,
"There are no straight lines in nature,
so how can there be squares?"
    "Imaginatively, hypothetically, in play."
After the building blocks of man topple
the infinite lines of bending light
will still be traveling still. Movement is
in our minds. Galaxies and hearts may not
move but swing, throb, obey.

All Summer my lovely wife complained.
When I asked her why, she said it was too hot.

When I asked my Winter wife why she scolded so,
She said it was too cold.

    This is why I deserted them
    for a Spring wife and for a wife of Fall.

At first it worked well
my Spring wife dancing and gay,
my wife in Fall in beauteous robes
and her embraces as feathers of silk.

But each summer my Spring wife disappeared
and in the winter my wife of Fall was nowhere to be found.

Thus summer and winter was I lonely
and spring and autumn, glad,
and I was but half alive,
living without a wife for half of each year.

Yet there was nothing to be done
for when a man chooses wives
he must endure his choices.

Nor could I find anyone who could tell me what to do
until one day wandering in a woodland
I came upon a hut with a sign over the door marked Sage.
Surely this sage will tell me, I thought.
So I asked him.

So he told me: Make a meeting of your four wives and ask them.
I wrote them letters they never answered.
This angered me so I went back and burned down the sage's hut
and of the ashes brewed a tea.
It had a sourish taste and as I drank it
I grew suddenly both hot and cold.
Sparks danced in my eyes and I could see
flowers growing quickly into buds.
Brilliant leaves fluttered from the ground
up on the trees.

How can I be hot and cold together, I wondered,
and how can flowers become buds and colored leaves turn green again?
I felt as if all my wives were singing with me
and there was nothing to be gained or lost
and no seasons nor birth nor death
nor any pain or pleasure.

It is like this in the center of sun, the sage seemed
to be explaining,
for from here your wives have issued forth

and from here day and night begin and everything human and natural.
Enveloped in a white light
I was much more than someone with four wives.
Now all women were wives and all men as myself
and this a great mystery.

If it had not been for my wives
I might never have met the sage
and if I had not met the sage I
would never have burned down his hut
and made tea and entered sun
and known all beings as one.

Does this seem dreamlike or strange?
Is life out of water strange   to the fish?
Is flying in air strange to the worm?
Of course.
Yet beings live out of water
and fly above earth
and some men have four wives and more.
And though they may not know it yet
humans see and feel and move
as light.

REJUVENATION AND LONG LIFE

can be yours now
through a secret 5,000 years old

Do you want to live younger and longer?

If your answer is yes, here is the way to do it. Not theory, not history, or conjecture, or one man's opinion about it, not scientific doubletalk—but exactly how to do it.

George Ohsawa who has been traveling the world teaching this method for 40 years has written over 200 books on the subject. They are all condensed into these few pages approved by him.

Few persons have the time to read long books. Anyone has the time to grow younger.

Would you like to feel better than you have in years?

Do this:

Pour two cups of water over a cup of brown rice, bring to a boil; turn down and simmer until the rice has absorbed the water. Make this your food for two to ten days. Take nothing else.

Or, before cooking add a little sea salt, vegetables, and fish if you wish. Then chew slowly, very slowly and considerately, digesting the food in the mouth. Also reduce your liquid intake as much as possible. The brown rice already has ample liquidity.

What happens?

1) *From the first meal, this nectar soothes you inners.*
2) *Providing bulk, it helps your elimination.*
3) *It defats.*
4) *It nourishes.*
5) *It absorbs and eliminates systemic poisons.*

To verify, eat the brown rice without meat, potatoes, yeasted breads, canned, sprayed or artificially treated foods, and take no medicines, vitamins, liquors, sweet drinks, juices. And no sugar.

If desired you may vary the rice or mix it with buckwheat, wheat, oats, barley, corn, millet—foods that have sustained whole civilizations for over 5,000 years.

Eat only when hungry and stop eating when still hungry. Increase the sea salt (obtainable in "health" food stores) to stop the sweet craving. Then diminish it since too much salt calls for too much liquid.

This, in brief, outlines the macrobiotic rejuvenating method of George Ohsawa as practiced by thousands of persons over the world as a result of his 40 years of teaching it.

It is based on the yin-yang transformative philosophy of China with rice as a best-balanced food, approximately 5 potassium (yin) to 1 sodium (yang). We usually swing between too yin or too yang not only in foods but in other behavior—pessimistic-optimistic, negative-positive, underactive-overactive.

You may read about it in detail in his book in Japanese, English, French, German: Ohsawa Foundation, 8 Kasumi-cho, Azabu, Minato-ku, Tokyo, Japan, and in macrobiotic restaurants in New York, Paris, Tokyo, and elsewhere.

Why should such a germinal seed method have us feeling better and flexible rather than stiff, younger instead of older? Greens of earth absorb the minerals. Creatures eat the greens as seeds, mutating hemoglobin (blood) from chlorophyl. If I can eat 13,500 opening (cooked) seeds a day (1½ cups of brown rice), my trillion cells enjoy it. One herb yielding seed buds into 10,000. It is the source of my potential energy and joy.

This most precious secret has been known since man discovered fire and salt and built his civilizations because of them. Over in Japan and China one can still hear, "If you are sick, just eat brown rice."

Try it.

No one can do this for you. Do what? Discover the spirit of life.

We are nothing but something, the transformation of grasses, children of seeds. Our human seed grows three billion times in weight in nine months, but twenty times after birth. The invisible life becomes visible.

Something immeasurably great unchanges in change, something we don't see, infinity. Self changes continually in our relative world in alternations of magnetic-electric, night-day, yin-yang, receptive-impressive. It is up to us to get in rhythm with this change just as we do with the seasons.

The miracle of a tiny seed unfolding into a tree or a tree packaging into a perfect seed is possible because of an unborn state contracting and expanding into seed and tree.

We are finite because of our infinite, our ever being. Surely our sustenance and our thanks spring from here.

1.   CUP OF RICE—To one cup of brown rice add about two cups of water, bring to a boil, turn down and simmer until the rice has absorbed the water. Let it stand. Do not cook in aluminum or in enamel that has cracked.

2.   SESAME SALT — Add a pinch of sea salt before cooking. When serving, use a pinch of sesame salt to taste. Sesame salt is made by toasting sesame seeds and adding sea salt in a proportion of 1 salt to 5 sesame seeds and crushing them fine. One also may season with soy sauce made without sugar. If you have thirst, you have taken to much salt.

3.   VEGETABLES—Cook vegetables in with the brown rice or sauté them and eat separately as dandelion, cress, carrots, pumpkin, parsley, onion, radish, cabbage, peas, spinach, etc., but not potatoes, tomatoes, or eggplant. Eat a quantity of nine-tenths brown rice and one-tenth vegetables for, at the most, less than one-third vegetables for a few months at least. The vegetables should be locally and organically grown and without chemical additives. Meat, canned foods, artificially prepared foods are to be avoided.

4.   HOW TO EAT—Eat when hungry. Do not eat when not hungry. Hunger is the best food. Chew and chew and chew and chew and chew. Digest the food in your mouth before swallowing. Poor foods are transmuted into good foods by chewing. Your foods will begin to taste better. So will you.

5.   HOW NOT TO EAT—Take no sugar and no sugar products. Avoid much fruit and take small amounts of fruit only when fully ripe, free from sprays, and grown locally in season.

6.   UNDER-EAT—The best food is little better than the worst if you over-eat. Under-eat. Never overeat.

7. EAT HAPPILY—Never eat if angry, resentful, fearful. Eating too can be a good way of living, simply, thankful, vitally.

8. EAT ANYTHING—Eat anything at all. Learn from what you eat if it is good for you. The brown rice will soon fortify you, make you more aware of what foods are doing to you after you eat them.

9. ACTIVATE—The Ancients had a good rule: No work, no food. *And, no joy, no food.*

10. REJUVENATE AND LIVE WELL AND LONG—Rejuvenation is possible. It is going on all the time. We make ourselves younger or older with the food we eat, the way we move, the way we think and feel.

Animals pause before eating to savor and sense. They stop eating when hunger is satisfied. We too have a good guide—our judgement, innate wisdom, intention.

Over the world there are many food fads and fashions. Over the centuries men have lived best on herbs bearing seeds. You may rediscover this old, old secret even if you are a city dweller out of touch with great nature.

Can you rejuvenate and live longer? The answer is *yes.* You are what you are eating, feeling, realing.

Zen Macrobiotics, the art of rejuvenation and longevity, $2.00 from the Japan address given above. Also another book, *The Philosophy of Oriental Medicine,* $4.00 postpaid.

George Ohsawa names his method Zen Rejuvenation and it is exactly that in Japan. Many who are sick go to the Zen monasteries to get well.

They eat very simply. Breakfast, a cup of rice gruel. Lunch, boiled barley and miso soup. Dinner, boiled barley or rice with a few vegetables. Other grains if on hand. They rise at 4 A.M. and have at least two hours a day of still sitting to quiet the mind and order the rhythms within, rhythms of nervestream, bloodstream, breathstream, internal rhythms probably derived from the sea and sun. There is chanting (to oxygenate) and always hard work in the fields or gardens (to activate the organism). You need not visit Japan to get these benefits.

If you wish to sit still, you may do so. In an upright balanced easeful position, release internal tensions including seeing and thinking. If you do this at regular periods daily for a shorter time than you wish, your rewards can be surprising, provided you don't make a business of it—you do it in sheer delight.

If you will activate, there are countless ways to work. The poor man often lives longer than the rich one because he is active. If you would chant and sing no one will stop you.

Self-dicipline as a philosophy has been written about in other books so extensively that Ohsawa focuses attention on our self-chemicalization through the food we eat and the way we eat it. If you choose to help your body make itself well, gradually, day by day, and feel better than you have in years, the eating manner has been given. Try it. If a bird can sing for joy but not you, eat seeds until you do!

How easy it is to get well when sick, simply by stopping doing the things that make us sick such as: over-eating, eating over-richly, overdrinking, drinking unsimple liquids, under-action and sluggishness, medicines, drugs, man-made vitamins, lack of honesty with ourselves, not enough appreciation of others, lack of understanding of cosmic and personal polarity in balance —in short, rebelliousness against great nature, our essential being.

And lack of appreciative chewing and predigesting of the foods we do eat.

Ohsawa is 71-years-old, but in the truth of living he is not over 55. The most alive, most vibrant men and women I have met on earth have been brown-rice eaters.

The American Indians who migrated from the Orient into North and South America cultivated corn as a basic seed food. Mexicans today are remarkably happy people with corn and wheat as their mainstay. Over in China, India, and the entire Orient millions of persons live on rice and wheat and live well, unless there are too many of them or their particular soil area has been exhausted.

Not only for 5,000 years but for a much longer time seed grains have sustained human life. The first page of the Bible says herbs bearing seed are to be our sustenance.

If hundreds of pages of personal experiences and testimonies followed these words as they might, you would not be any closer to rejuvenating, and perhaps less close for turning the simple matter into complex conjecture.

Testimonials always involve suffering and recovery from suffering. There is no need to put suffering in our mind at all. Let's leave it out. Let's cut our food costs in half, our cooking labors in half, our concern over foods in half. Let's double our energy and vitality and apply it to worthwhile works on earth. Let's eat thousands of seeds each day.

SQUARE
SUN
SQUARE
MOON
SQUARE
SUN
SQUARE
MOON
SQUARE
SUN
SQUARE
MOON
SQUARE
SUN
SQUARE
MOON
SQUARE
SUN
SQUARE
MOON
SQUARE
SUN
SQUARE
MOON
SQUARE
SUN
SQUARE
MOON
SQUARE
SUN
SQUARE
MOON
SQUARE
SUN
SQUARE
MOON

Other books by Reps:

ZEN FLESH ZEN BONES
ZEN TELEGRAMS
PICTURE-POEM PRIMER
UNWRINKLING PLAYS